Sew Like Knitting– A New Technique

Simply put, *Sew Like Knitting* is a unique method for creating garments and accessories from fabric. It requires only very basic cutting and sewing skills and results in finished pieces that look as if they were hand-knit.

"Thank goodness, I don't have to learn how to knit," exclaimed a quilt-shop owner when she saw the *Sew Like Knitting* technique. Sewers and quilters are always thrilled to discover that they can use this new fiber art to create the look and texture of knitting using fabric in tandem with their rotary-cutting tools, sewing machine, washer and dryer. It's so easy to transform fabric into a project that most people will think was hand-knit.

Sew Like Knitting is easy, fun and rewarding and grew out of my interests in fine arts, fabric, sewing, designing and teaching. The technique is the result of merging multiple skills and separate interests to create something uniquely my own. The technique is also a wonderful discovery that marries two loves: the look of knitting and designing patterns for multilayered, natural-fiber chenille fabrics and garments. Truth be told, I'm a klutz with knitting needles, but give me a sewing machine and fabric and I'm off to the races!

My husband was also instrumental in the development of this process. When I was in my early 30s, he encouraged me to do what I wanted to use my fine arts training and all my other related interests. He said, "You only go 'round once; figure out what you want to do and do it." So I did. During my studies at the University of Manitoba, I learned to throw traditional rules to the wind. And my fine arts studies certainly contributed to my off-the-wall, open-minded approach to sewing.

Technically, making chenille requires "deconstructing" layered-and-stitched fabrics by slashing the layers between rows of stitching and washing the results to create the characteristic napped surface. When you slash the layers between the rows of stitching, it is essential not to slash the bottommost layer. "Otherwise," as I used to laughingly say in my chenille classes, "you've got yourself a knitting project!" Little did I know how that statement would take root in an entirely new method grounded in the chenille technique.

Necessity provokes new inventions and *Sew Like Knitting* is a good example. The "Sewing Goddess" must have been smiling down on me one day two years ago when the proverbial lightbulb went on. You see, my husband and I were to attend a special outdoor event for our anniversary. I thought I had the perfect outfit, but when the weather proved to be too hot for it, I knew I needed a sleeveless dress (I had one) and a light wrap (I didn't have one). With only a day to come up with one, I instinctivly cut bias strips and sewed them to a grid on paper to create a lightweight shawl with the look of knitted lattice. *Sew Like Knitting* had taken wing without a knitting needle in sight.

I am delighted to be able to share this technique and all the new ideas that I have explored in the past two years to create unique projects for *Sew Like Knitting*. As the song says, I feel like I've "only just begun." This is just the first project book with more in the works.

Carol

Carol Moffatt

WARNING: Sew Like Knitting may become habit-forming!

Sew Like Knitting—A New Technique

Sew Like Knitting Projects

This is a project book of designs that appeal to women of all ages. As you try the different projects, you will learn new techniques. Like knitting, the techniques included are referred to as "stitches." If you love to sew with natural-fiber fabrics, you will love exploring the endless color, fabric and texture combinations you can create with *Sew Like Knitting*.

Each featured project was designed to look like a knit. If someone actually asks you for the knitting pattern and you surprise them when you tell them you made the garment you are wearing, then pat yourself on the back. You've succeeded!

To learn the basic technique, begin with Angela's Neck Lace, or try the easy Long & Lacy Scarf. These two projects introduce you to the essential steps while you create fun and functional projects.

Once you've mastered the basics, move on to the Sampler Scarf. It includes a number of techniques so that you can experience a few of the many texture possibilities *Sew Like Knitting* offers to the creative sewer. In fact, if you flip to pages 20-26, you can take a peek at color photos of some of the many "stitches" as well as before and after samples of the *Sew Like Knitting* process. Three poncos designs are also included as well as a pretty wrap and a cute little shrug that doubles as a chunky scarf.

Try the Multicolor Striped Wrap or Just a Little Shrug after you have warmed up to the technique with one of the easier projects. Then make the "piece de resistance," the Variegated Plaid Poncho.

As with any sewing project, it is essential to follow the directions. Take your time and have fun!

Sew Like Knitting Tools

You will need some basic sewing and cutting tools and a few things that are not quite as common. Make sure you have everything on hand before you begin.

- Rotary cutter with a sharp blade and extras (you will be doing a lot of cutting)
- 6 x 24-inch rotary ruler with a 45-degree-angle line
- 24 x 36-inch or larger cutting mat
- Optional: *Sew Like Knitting Cutting Grid* and temporary spray adhesive for fabric
- Tissue paper or other easy-to-tear stabilizer for the stitching foundation; fine-point pen and ruler or *Sew Like Knitting Sewing Grid Type A* and temporary spray adhesive
- Tray for fabric strips, such as a box lid or cookie sheet
- 90/14 universal or Microtex sewing machine needles
- Sewing scissors for clipping threads
- Long straight pins with heads (quilter's pins available from www.clotilde.com)
- Cotton osnaberg fabric or other coarse-weave, natural-fiber fabric as directed for the individual projects (See Fabric Selection below.)
- All-purpose sewing thread to match fabrics (See SLicK TRICK to the right.)
- Optional: Open-toe presser foot for sewing machine
- Sewing machine
- Lint roller

Sew Like Knitting Fabric Selection

In order to create the *Sew Like Knitting* textures ***you must use washable woven fabrics made of natural fibers:*** cotton, linen, rayon, silk or blends of natural fibers.

Woven cotton (with a coarse weave) is my fabric of choice because it is readily available, relatively inexpensive and easy to handle. My current favorite is osnaberg. (It may also be referred to as Waterford cotton.) Osnaberg becomes as soft as fur when you use it for a *Sew Like Knitting* project.

This cotton fabric is very durable and has a characteristic coarse weave; it resembles some linen fabrics. If the color you want is not readily available in osnaberg, you can dye it, but be sure to use a dye fixative to ensure colorfastness.

I suggest you use osnaberg or something similar with a coarse weave for your first *Sew Like Knitting* project. Then experiment with some of the others in the list for your next one if you choose. ***Note:*** *When using fabrics other than osnaberg, be sure to make a test sample before starting your project.* Otherwise, proceed at your own risk.

SLicK TRICK: Test the Thread

To ensure the thread is strong enough, wrap a piece around your index finger and pull with your other hand. If the thread breaks, choose a better-quality thread. Strong thread is an essential part of the project, as it literally holds the project together!

To make a test sample to ensure the desired results, you will need a ¼-yard cut of the fabric(s) in question. To test any fabric you want to use, follow the Test It directions at the end of each of the five essential steps for *Sew Like Knitting*. ***Note:*** *Be sure to read all of the essential steps before you begin, and refer to them as needed while you make your project.*

Sew Like Knitting Essential Steps

There are five basic steps to create each of the projects in this book. Occasionally, an additional step or two may be necessary before the final step (washing and drying). Each essential step is discussed in detail below. Refer back to these steps as needed while working on your projects.

STEP ONE: CUT THE FABRIC STRIPS

1. Press the fabric and fold in half lengthwise with selvages even. Make a short clip at the fold at one end and rip or cut the piece into two equal-size pieces (Piece #1 and Piece #2).

2. Place Piece #1 wrong side up on the rotary-cutting mat. Apply a light coat of temporary spray adhesive (optional) to adhere the fabric layers and keep them in place for accuracy while you cut.

3. Matching the torn edges (the true straight of grain), position Piece #2 on top of Piece #1, with wrong sides together. Smooth out any wrinkles.

4. Choose one of the two strip-cutting methods below. For either method, you will need the rotary cutter, mat and ruler. For Method One, you will measure each cut as you cut the entire piece into ⅝-inch-wide bias strips. If you choose Method Two, you will use the printed *Sew Like Knitting Cutting Grid* and temporary spray adhesive to save time. This method requires minimal measuring.

Method One: Measure & Cut Every Strip

1. Position the 45-degree-angle line on the ruler along the torn edges of the layered fabric. Cut along the ruler edge to make a 45-degree-angle cut edge on the fabric (Fig. 1).

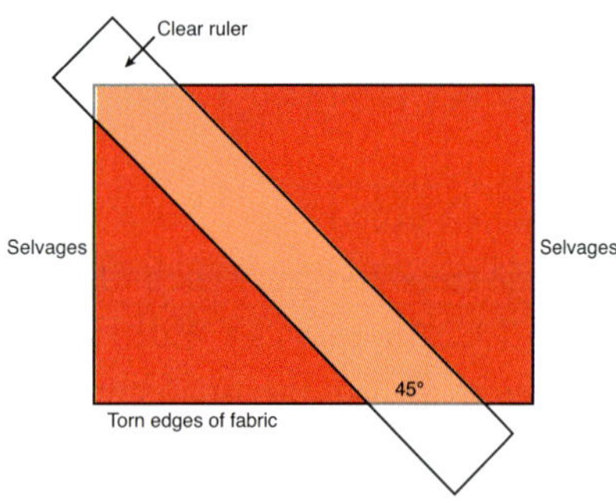

Fig. 1
Cutting Method One
Measure and cut every strip.

2. Measure ⅝ inch from the cut edge and then cut the required number of strips (see the cutting directions for the project you are making). ***Note:*** *To ensure strip-width accuracy, after every 10 cuts, position the 45-degree-angle line at the torn edges of the layered fabrics.* ***If the cut edge of the fabric does not align with the ruler edge,*** *make a cleanup cut before continuing to cut the next 10 strips.*

3. Trim all strip ends as shown so that all four cut edges are on the bias (Fig. 2). Place the layered strips on the tray.

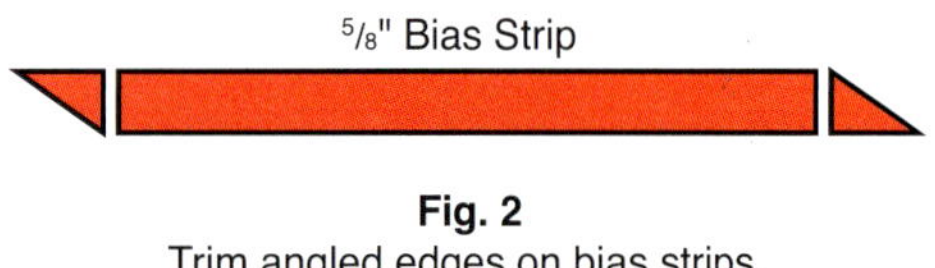

Fig. 2
Trim angled edges on bias strips.

Method Two: Use Sew Like Knitting Cutting Grid

1. Unfold the *Sew Like Knitting Cutting Grid* (printed tissue) and use a warm dry iron to remove any creases or wrinkles. Examine the grid. You will find dotted lines spaced ⅝ inch apart. These are cutting lines. Use the solid lines for lining up the straight grain of the fabric with the straight grain of the paper grid. Cut the grid in half at the centerline, where the angles of the dotted lines change on the paper (Fig. 3).

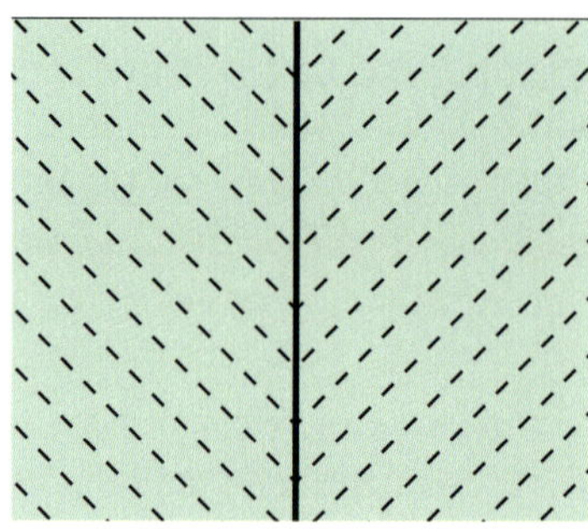

Fig. 3
Sew Like Knitting Cutting Grid (facsimile)

2. Trim one half-sheet of the grid to match the size of fabric Piece #2. ***Note:*** *The width of a half-sheet of cutting grid and the torn length of fabric are about the same. If the fabric is longer than a half-sheet, extend it as needed by cutting and taping a strip from the remaining half-sheet of gridded paper to one edge.*

3. Apply a light coat of temporary spray adhesive to the right side of fabric Piece #2. Place the cutting grid on top, lining up the solid line on the grid with the torn edge (straight of grain). Smooth the paper into place, eliminating any wrinkles.

4. Cut strips from the gridded fabric layers using your rotary-cutting tools. Begin at one corner of the sheet and cut on the dotted lines. Cut as many strips as specified in the directions for your project (Fig. 4).

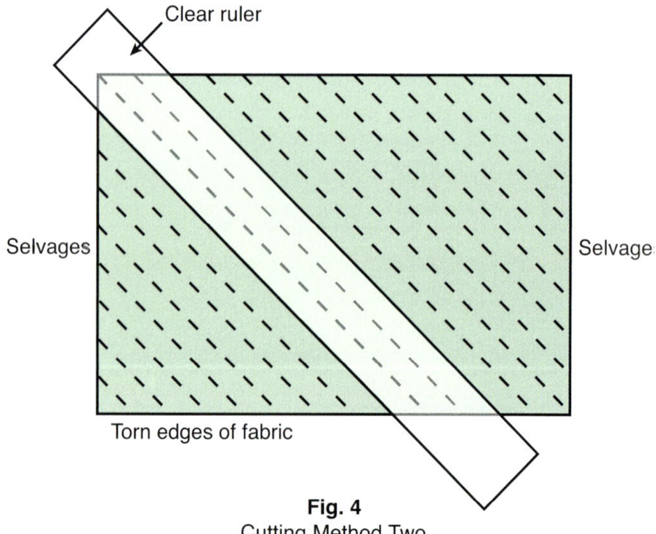

Fig. 4
Cutting Method Two
Use Sew Like Knitting cutting grid.

5. Carefully remove and discard the paper strips and cut the ends as shown in Fig. 2. Place the strips on the tray so they are arranged in order from the shortest to the longest.

Test It: Cut ⅝-inch-wide true-bias strips from ¼ yard of fabric using your choice of Method One or Method Two as described above.

STEP TWO: CREATE THE SEWING GRID

Next, choose the method you will use to sew the strips to the grid and prepare the sewing grid for your project. You can make your own sewing grid or use a sheet of *Sew Like Knitting Sewing Grid.*

Method One: Create Your Own Sewing Grid

1. Choose tear-away stabilizer or tissue paper to make your grid. Test the paper first to make sure it will be easy to remove. To do so, first adjust the sewing machine for a short stitch (1.5mm). Place a short strip of the layered fabric on the paper and stitch through the center. The paper should be sturdy enough to resist tearing during stitching and should be easy to tear away.

2. To prepare the paper foundation for your project, use a ruler and fine-point pen to draw an accurate 1¼-inch grid on the paper. For long or large projects, you may need to tape two or more sheets of paper or stabilizer together to create a grid of the correct size for the project you are making. Refer to the project directions for the grid size (the number of squares across and down).

SLicK TRICK

Make It Easy!

Number the squares on the paper in both directions (Fig. 5).

1	2	3	4	5	6
2					
3					
4					
5					
6					

Fig. 5
Number squares in both directions.

Method Two: Use Sew Like Knitting Sewing Grid

The printed 43 x 56-inch sewing grids for *Sew Like Knitting* projects were designed to maintain accuracy and save time. Two styles are available. The projects in this book require only type A.

Type A is a square grid with 1¼-inch squares. The projects in this book require only Type A sheets.

Type B is printed with a diagonal grid of 1-inch squares.

1. Each project will direct you to cut a grid of a specific size and shape with the number of squares across and down. Be sure to trim away the rectangles around the outer edges of the printed grid before you begin so the grid is 32 x 42 squares.

2. If the sheet is not large enough for the size or shape specified in the project directions, cut another sheet that is one square wider or longer than the required addition and overlap the two by one square before taping them together. Make sure that the grid lines on the two sheets are accurately aligned.

Test It: Cut out or draw a 6-square sewing grid.

SLicK TRICK

Master It!

Draw a master grid on a heavyweight paper using a fine-tip felt pen. When you start a new project, make your own sewing grid by placing a fresh sheet of tissue or stabilizer over the master. The other option is to purchase a package of the *Sew Like Knitting Sewing Grid* and set aside one sheet each of Type A and Type B to use as your master sheet.

Optional: To preserve it and make it stronger for re-use, fuse lightweight interfacing to the back of a sheet and hang on a clip-style hanger in your sewing closet to keep it as wrinkle-free as possible.

STEP THREE: SEW THE STRIPS TO THE SEWING GRID
You will be directed to use ***Single Strips*** or ***Double Strips*** in the step-by-step directions for your project. Some projects require both.

Single Strip: A bias-cut strip. When you cut the bias strips as directed above, they will be in pairs. Separate the pairs into ***Single Strips***.

Double Strip: Two layered strips. Since you cut the strips double-layer in Step One, these are ready to go when ***Double Strips*** are specified in the project directions.

Test the Stitch & Tension

Before sewing the strips to the grid as directed, adjust the sewing machine for a shorter-than-normal stitch length (1.5–1.8mm or 10–12 stitches per inch) and test the tension. It is essential to use a shorter stitch and a strong thread because the stitching is what holds everything together in the finished piece. *Testing is essential.*

1. Choose a strip at least 5 inches long; position it on a line on a small piece of the sewing grid or on a line drawn on a scrap of tissue. Stitch in place through the center of the strip. *Do not backstitch at the beginning or end of the row.* Leave a long bobbin-thread tail at the end of the stitching.

2. Examine the stitching on both sides. Adjust the tension if necessary to create a balanced stitch. ***Note:*** *You can test this by pulling on the bobbin thread. If you can pull it out easily, the top tension is too loose or the bobbin tension is too tight. Try loosening the top tension and test again.*

3. When the tension is balanced, pull the bobbin thread again, and if it breaks easily, replace with a better-quality, stronger thread.

4. Test-sew through two layers of strips; you may need to adjust the tension again. ***Note:*** *Do not underestimate the importance of testing stitch length and tension. Strong thread is an essential part of the project, as it literally holds the project together!*

5. Sew the strips to the grid using one of the two methods below. Test both methods first to decide which works best for you.

Method One: Pin the Strips to the Grid

Some sewers find it easier to pin the strips to the grid lines before sewing.

1. Place the sewing grid right side up on a large flat surface.

2. Referring to the project directions, position strips on the sewing grid in the direction indicated (short or long lines). Pin in place, placing the pins in the center of the strips and parallel to the cut edges, with all pins pointing in the same direction. The strip ends should begin and end *beyond* both edges of the grid. If the strips are not long enough to complete the grid line, add a second strip, lapping it over the end of the first strip by at least ½ inch (Fig. 6).

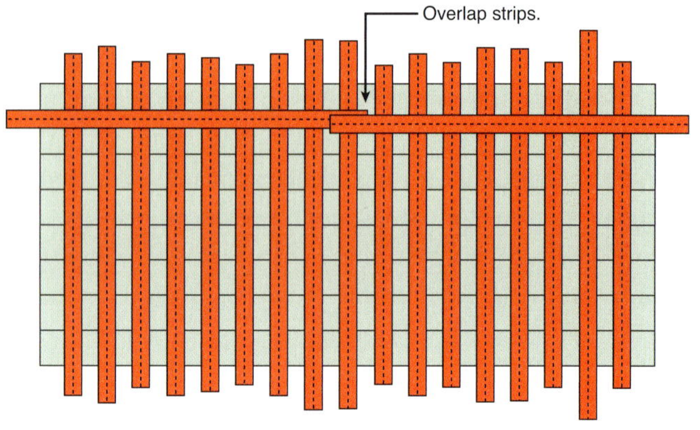

Fig. 6
Lap strips by ½"–1" when strips are not long enough to cover the grid lines.

3. Arrange the pinned sheet with the pin points toward the upper edge and carefully roll it up from the left, leaving only the first six rows exposed.

4. Position the roll so that the points of the pins are facing the sewing machine, making it easy to pull them out as you reach them. Beginning and ending the stitching in the excess strip, sew the first strip to the grid through the center, removing the pins as you stitch. Do not backstitch. Unroll the grid as needed to stitch all remaining strips in the same manner.

5. After sewing strips in one direction, pin and sew strips in the opposite direction, creating a fabric grid (Fig. 7).

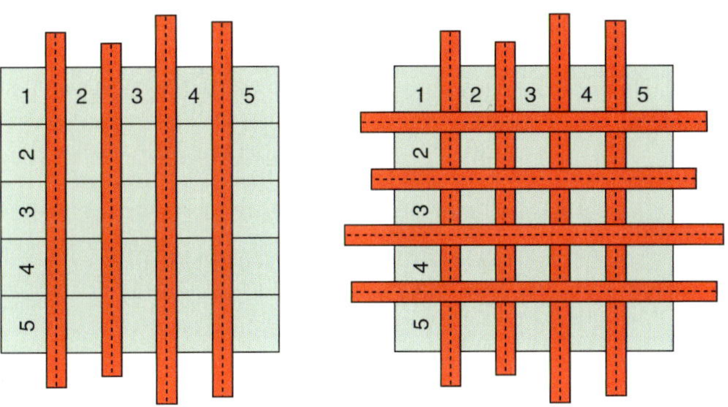

Fig. 7
Sew strips to grid in one direction and then the other.

SLicK TRICK

Don't Forget!

If you are sewing on a computerized machine and must interrupt your sewing session by turning off the machine, put a little note on the front of your machine to remind yourself of the stitch length you are using. Turning your machine off and then turning it back on will give you the factory-set default length, and you will need to readjust the length to the one you determined was best when you started your project.

Method Two: Arrange & Sew As You Go

If you prefer not to use pins, you can position strips on the grid as you work from one end of the grid to the other. Here's how.

1. If the project is large, roll the grid from one edge, leaving only 6–10 lines showing.

2. Beginning at the exposed right-hand edge of the rolled grid, place a fabric strip on the first line indicated. Make sure the strip extends past both edges of the grid. Hold the strip in place over the line as you stitch through the center of the strip. Begin and end the stitching in the excess strip beyond both edges of the sewing grid. Do not backstitch.

3. Sew the strips to the lines indicated in the project. If a strip isn't long enough to cover a line, add another strip as shown in Fig. 6. After sewing all strips to the grid in one direction, repeat the process to add and sew the required strips to the grid lines in the opposite direction.

Test It: Sew the test strips onto all of the lines on the 5-inch square of sewing grid you cut earlier. Test ***Single Strips*** and ***Double Strips*** if your project requires both types.

STEP FOUR: REMOVE THE SEWING GRID

1. After sewing strips to the sewing grid or to the tissue or stabilizer grid you prepared, remove the paper. Because you tested it first (right?) and because the stitches are short, it should be easy to tear the tissue or stabilizer away from the needle perforations. See the SLicK TRICK on page 10 for help with removing paper grids.

2. Complete all sewing steps as directed for your project before moving on to Step Five. ***Note:*** *In a number of the featured projects, you will be directed to add more strips to the grid at this stage to create a denser fabric.*

Test It: Remove the paper from your test sample. For many projects, you will be directed to trim the excess strip ends even with the outermost strips before you proceed to the next step.

SLicK TRICK

Tug It!

To remove tissue-paper grids, including the Sew Like Knitting Sewing Grid, hold the stitched piece at both edges and tug gently to pull the paper away from the perforations; you will need to move down the length of the piece in both directions to tug all of the paper away from the stitches before lifting the paper away from the fabric strips. (Follow the instructions in the package.)

If there are small bits of the tissue or tear-away stabilizer left behind after the laundering process, use a tweezers to remove any pieces still trapped under the stitches. (You'll probably need to get out the vacuum cleaner when you're done!) Now you have a completed fabric grid with a right and wrong side.

STEP FIVE: WASH & DRY THE PROJECT

This is where the magic happens! All you need is your washing machine and dryer to make the stitched lattice grid "blossom" into a lovely textured web of fiber that resembles hand knitting.

Most automatic washing machines work well, but front-loading machines that have low agitation may not give the desired results. In that case, you may need to wash and dry the piece more than once for the desired effect. Adding a few other pieces to the wash—cloth rags, old jeans, or old towels, for example—will help improve the agitation. This is a linty process so it is essential to remove the threads from your washer and dryer after each step to avoid operational problems later. ***Note:*** *It is best to clean threads from the washing machine after the first spin cycle and again at the end of the wash. Be sure to clean the lint trap in your dryer before you dry the washed piece. Clean it again at mid-cycle and at the end of the drying cycle.*

Although this last step creates a lot of lint, I have not experienced any mechanical problems with my washing machine or dryer because I take the time to remove threads and lint periodically during both processes. You must take responsibility for using this process in your own machines to keep them in good working order.

Test It: Remove the paper or stabilizer grid and wash the lattice in the washing machine; dry in the dryer. It will be necessary to wash small sample pieces more than once to get the fabric edges to "blossom." If you are happy with the look of the sample, proceed with your first project.

Sew Like Knitting Fringe

Some projects in this book have fringe. In some, the fringe is built right into the construction—simply follow the directions and the fringe appears naturally in the finished item. Angela's Neck Lace, Poncho Asymmetric and the Multicolor Striped Wrap have built-in fringe. In some projects, you will add fringe (Figs. 8 and 9).

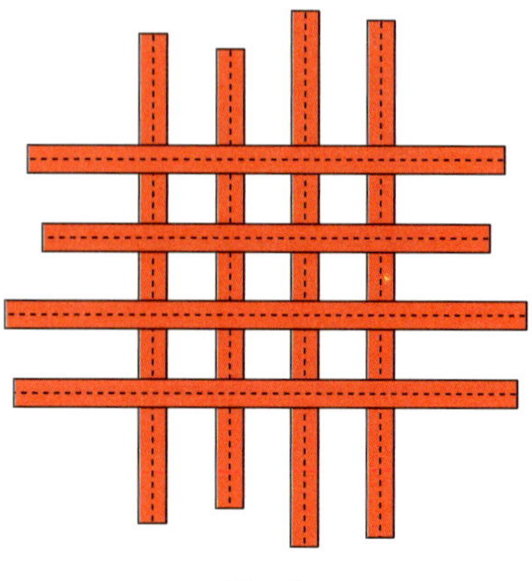

Fig. 8
Built-in Fringe

In both long scarf projects, strips are added to the ends of both scarves to create the (optional) fringe. When creating fringe strips, it is essential to follow the four basic *Sew Like Knitting* steps below. *You must stitch through the center of the fringe strips before you add them to the project.* Remember, *the stitching is what holds the washed threads together in the finished project.* Use the same stitch length you use for stitching strips to the grid. Some projects require ***Single Strips*** and others require ***Double Strips***.

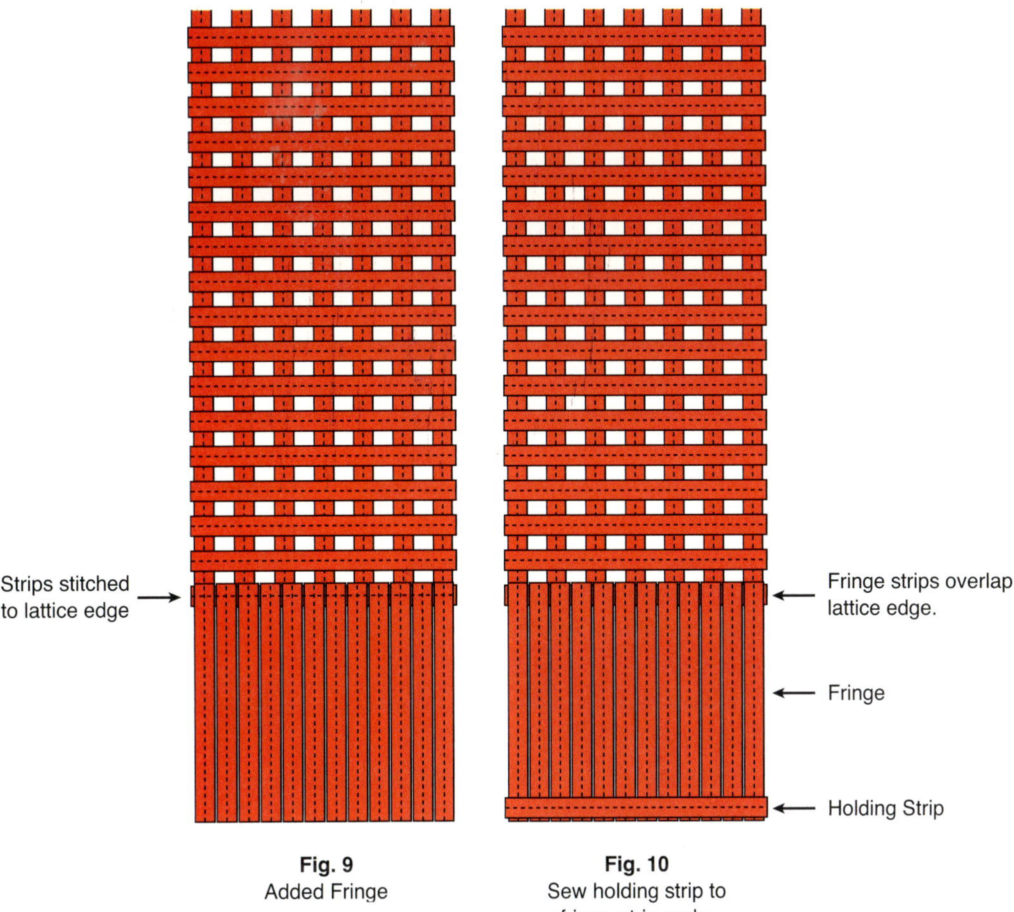

Fig. 9
Added Fringe

Fig. 10
Sew holding strip to fringe-strip ends.

To add fringe to a project:

1. Refer to the project directions and stitch through the center of ***Single*** or ***Double Strips*** as indicated.

2. Cut fringe strips to the length given in the project directions and stitch through the center of each one. Be sure to use ***Singles*** or ***Doubles*** as specified in the project directions.

3. To sew the fringe strips to the wrong side of the outermost strip (border) of the lattice, place one end of each strip across the width of the last strip at the end of the lattice and pin in place. If you prefer, you can position each fringe strip as you sew from one to the next. Fringe-strip spacing is your decision unless specified in the project directions.

4. After adding the fringe strips to the project edge, it is essential to anchor the loose ends by stitching them to another ***Single Strip*** (holding strip) so the fringe won't tangle when you wash and dry the project (Fig. 10).

SLicK TRICK

Back-Up Strips!

Make some extra strips while you are sewing your project. Set these aside for mending any undetected errors in the finished project. To make them, select a long strip from your tray of prepared strips and stitch through the center of the strip through all layers (one layer for ***Singles*** and two for ***Doubles***). For storage purposes, overlap the short ends of each strip and stitch to create a circle. Wash and dry the circle with the project. Leave the washed strip in a circle to store and prevent tangling until you are ready to use it. Then cut it apart at the stitching. If your project requires different fabrics and colors and ***Single*** and ***Double Strips***, make a back-up strip of each one.

Sew Like Knitting Q & A

Q: How do I know if I should use ***Single*** or ***Double Strips***?
A. Read through the directions for your project. Remember that this technique is similar to knitting. If you change yarns, you get different results. If you use a fabric different from the one shown in the project, your results may vary. Always make a 10- or 12-inch test square with strips of your intended fabrics to be sure you will be happy with the results. For clothing and accessories, I prefer **Single** *or* **Double strips**. *The directions for each project indicate the strip type(s) required.*

Q: What do I do if my sample shrinks?
A: To prevent shrinkage, it's always a good idea to preshrink (wash and dry) the fabric before you test it or use it in a project. With some projects, like Angela's Neck Lace and the Long & Lacy Scarf, sizing isn't really an issue, but it's still a good idea to make a test sample so you will know what you will get when the finished project comes out of the dryer.

Q: What do I do if my sample is larger after it has been washed and dried?
A: Remember that bias stretches. Projects made of bias-cut strips of loosely woven natural fibers can grow rather than shrink in size. To determine if this could be a potential problem for garments where size is important, prepare a test sample 10–12 inches square and measure it before the laundering process. When dry, smooth it out and measure it to determine if it has grown. If it has, use this fabric type for the first three projects where size in not an issue. The only way to ensure that the project will come out exactly as illustrated is to follow the directions precisely, using the fabric specified.

Q: What do I do if the paper sewing grid rips while I am sewing?
A: If this happens on every single row you stitch, lengthen the stitch and make another test sample. Occasionally, the grid will tear in places while you work due to the growing weight with the added fabric strips. It's important to keep the grid intact until you are ready to remove it. Stop when you notice a tear and repair it before proceeding. Turn the work over, coax the edges of the tear together and secure with small pieces of cellophane tape.

Q: My sewing veered off center in some of the strips. Do I have to undo the stitching and redo it?
A: It's OK if you wander off center occasionally. If, however, your stitching is close to the edge of the strip as shown in Fig. 11, carefully trim the strip away only in the area where the stitching is too close to the edge and discard it. Position a new strip on the grid line over the remnants of the first strip with ends overlapping by at least ½ inch as shown earlier in Fig. 6. Stitch in place. Trust me, the patch job will not be visible in the finished project.

Stitching is slightly off center, but OK to use.

Stitching is too close to one edge. Remove and replace.

Fig. 11
Check stitching on strips.

Q: What do I do with the bias-strip leftovers?
A: Save leftovers in clear bags or containers, sorted and labeled by color and length, to use in future projects. Leftovers are perfect for the Confetti Poncho on page 31.

Q: How do I repair any holes in the finished project
A: If there is a hole in a project when it comes out of the dryer, it can be easily repaired by positioning a back-up strip (see page 11) across the open area. Lap both ends of the back-up strip over the "hole" by ½ inch. Stitch in place on top of the previous stitching.

Q: How do I replace missing fringe?
A: Cut a back-up strip to the fringe length given in the project directions. Pin to the project where a fringe strip is missing and stitch in the same manner you added fringe during the project construction. Backstitch at the beginning and end of the stitching.

The Sew Like Knitting Projects

Angela's Neck Lace

This easy project was inspired by a beautiful silk ribbon "scarflette." It has its own built-in fringed edge, and you can make it and wear it in just a few hours—an easy way to get familiar with this easy technique.

PROJECT SPECIFICATIONS

Finished Size: **15 inches square**
Skill Level: **Easy**

MATERIALS

- ¾ yard 45-inch-wide natural-fiber woven fabric such as cotton osnaberg
- Optional: *Sew Like Knitting Cutting Grid* and temporary spray adhesive
- Tray for fabric strips
- All-purpose thread to match fabric
- ½ sheet *Sew Like Knitting Cutting Grid Type A* (1¼-inch squares) OR 23-inch square of tear-away stabilizer or tissue paper and fine-tip pen and ruler
- Rotary cutter, mat and ruler
- Open-toe presser foot for sewing machine
- Lint roller
- Basic sewing tools and equipment

INSTRUCTIONS

***Project Note:** All bias strips in this project are **Single Strips**.* *See Step One on page 5.*

1. Prepare the fabric as directed in Step One on page 5. Cut the layered fabric into ⅝-inch-wide bias strips and cut off the angled ends as shown in Fig. 2 on page 6. Separate the layers so you have ***Single Strips***.

2. Cut 28 of the strips to at least 16 inches long for the lines on the grid and place on the tray. Set the remaining strips to one side on the tray.

3. ***To use the Sew Like Knitting Sewing Grid Type A,*** cut a 12 x 12 grid of squares. ***To make your own sewing grid***, draw a 12 x 12 grid of 1¼-inch squares on tissuepaper or tear-away stabilizer. Number the squares in both directions. Draw a diagonal line from the upper corner of the upper left square to the lower right corner of square 9/9 as shown in Fig. 1. Repeat on the wrong side of the sewing grid.

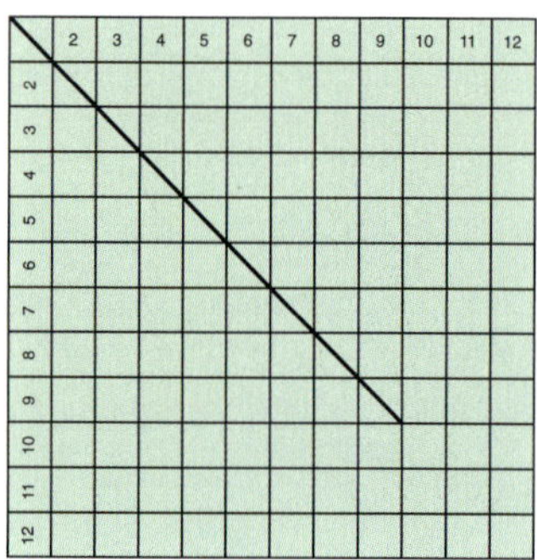

Fig. 1
Prepare the sewing grid.

Make It Confetti

To create a confetti effect like that of the Confetti Poncho as shown here, you will need a 22½-inch-long, true-bias ***Single Strip*** of a contrasting color. Cut this strip into ½-inch-long pieces.

When adding the second set of strips to the sewing grid, position a contrasting piece on top at each strip intersection. See block 9 of Confetti Poncho on page 25.

4. Adjust the sewing machine stitch length to 1.5mm and test the tension as directed on page 8.

5. Center and pin a 16-inch-long ***Single Strip*** over the first horizontal line, allowing excess strip to extend beyond the edges of the sewing grid. Sew through the center of the strip, beginning and ending the stitching on the excess strip. Add strips to the remaining horizontal rows in the same manner. Position and stitch a strip to each vertical row (Fig. 2).

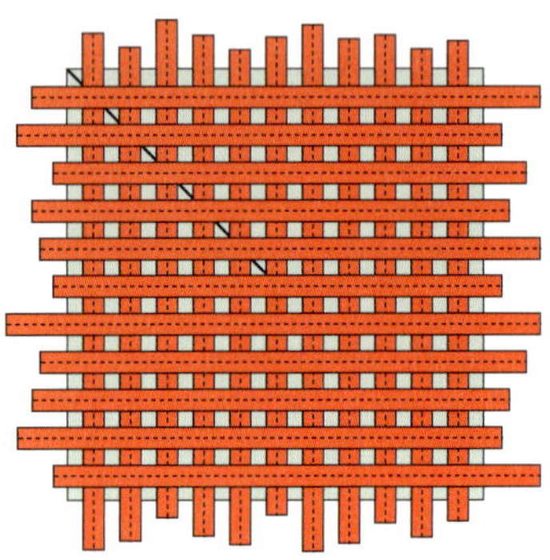

Fig. 2
Sew strips to grid.

6. Flip the piece wrong side up and cut through the diagonal line you drew (step 3) to create the neckline opening.

7. Turn the piece right side up. Position the raw edge of a ***Single Strip*** at each neckline opening edge and stitch through the center (Fig. 3).

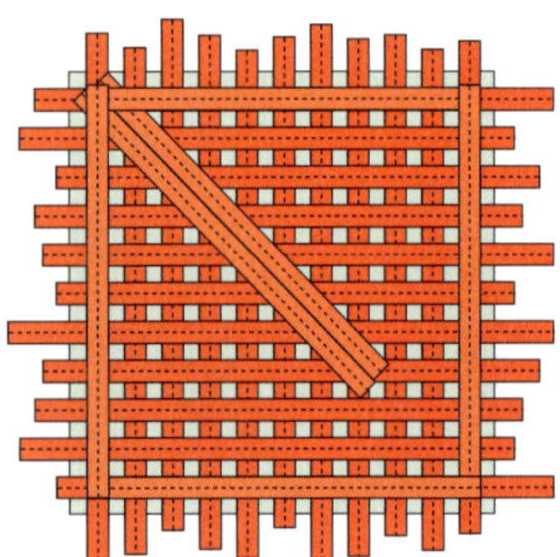

Fig. 3
Sew strips to neckline edge and outermost lattice strips.

8. Trim the excess strips even with the grid edges as shown in Fig. 4.

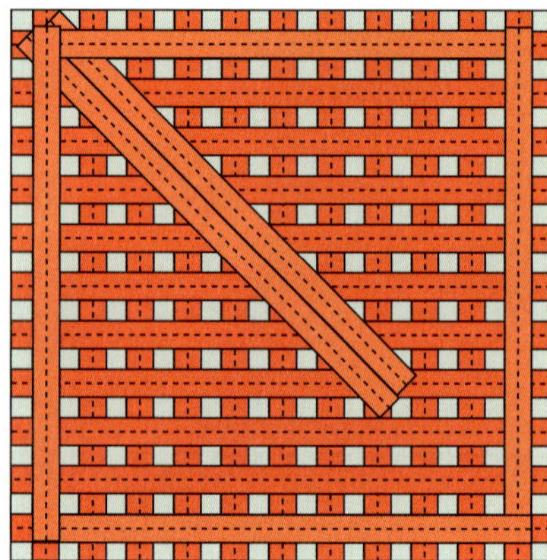

Fig. 4
Trim strips even with the edge of the grid.

9. Remove the paper or stabilizer grid as directed on page 9.

10. The strip ends that extend beyond the border strips create the fringe. Flip the piece over to the wrong side and pin and sew ***Single Strips*** to the outer strips all the way around the piece to reinforce the border. They will lie behind the border strips you added in step 7.

11. Trim any loose threads and place the fabric grid in the washing machine with an old towel or jeans. Wash and dry as directed in Step Five on page 10, stopping the cycle twice to remove lint during both cycles. If the resulting "neck lace" doesn't "blossom" as much as desired, repeat this step.

12. Remove the piece from the dryer and shake outside to remove loose lint or threads. Run a lint roller over it to remove any remaining lint.

13. To wear the completed piece, try tying it to one side at the shoulder. ●

Long & Lacy Scarf

This scarf is an easy project for one of your first *Sew Like Knitting* experiences. It was inspired by the chunky knit scarves that are all the current rage. No one will guess it isn't a knit. You will learn the basic technique, plus how to add fringe.

PROJECT SPECIFICATIONS

Finished Size: 7½ x 94 inches, including fringe
Skill Level: Easy

MATERIALS

- 1 yard 45-inch-wide red cotton osnaberg or other similar woven natural-fiber fabric
- Optional: *Sew Like Knitting Cutting Grid* and temporary spray adhesive
- Tray for fabric strips
- All-purpose thread to match fabric
- 1 yard 23-inch-wide tear-away stabilizer or tissue paper and a fine-tip pen and ruler OR ½ sheet of *Sew Like Knitting Cutting Grid Type A* (1¼-inch squares)
- Rotary cutter, mat and ruler
- Open-toe presser foot for sewing machine
- Clear cellophane tape
- Lint roller
- Basic sewing tools and equipment

INSTRUCTIONS

Project Note: *All bias strips in this project are* ***Single Strips****. See Step One on page 5.*

1. Prepare the fabric as directed in step 1 on page 5. Cut the layered fabric into ⅝-inch-wide bias strips and cut off the angled ends as shown in Fig. 2 on page 6. Separate into ***Single Strips***.

2. Before placing strips on the tray, trim 65 strips to 10–12-inch lengths for the short lines on the grid. Place all strips on the tray.

3. *To use the Sew Like Knitting Sewing Grid Type A,* cut two pieces, each 8 x 34 squares; tape together to create a strip that measures 8 x 67 squares (see Step Two, page 7). *To make your own sewing grids,* draw a grid of 8 x 67 (1¼-inch) squares on the tear-away stabilizer or tissue.

4. Adjust the sewing machine for a 1.5mm stitch length and test the tension as directed on page 8.

5. Center and pin the short ***Single Strips*** to the grid on the short lines with excess strip extending at each edge (see Step Three, page 8). Beginning at one short end, roll the grid so approximately 10 rows of squares are showing, and pin the rolled layers together.

Long & Lacy Scarf

6. Sew through the center of each strip, beginning and ending the stitching on the excess fabric strip beyond the edges of the sewing grid. Unroll and re-pin the grid as needed until you have stitched all remaining strips in place in this direction.

7. After you have stitched all the short strips to the grid, sew strips to the long grid lines in the same manner. If some of your bias strips are too short, simply overlap a second strip by at least ½ inch and continue stitching as shown in Fig. 1.

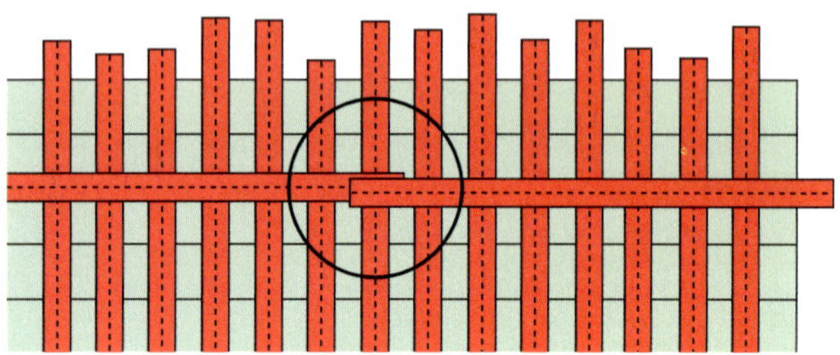

Fig. 1
Overlap strips to fill grid lines as needed.

8. Remove the paper or stabilizer grid as directed in Step Four on page 9.

9. Place the scarf on the cutting mat and trim the ends and edges so the resulting scarf is 6 squares wide x 65 squares long. The outer edges of the scarf will be referred to as the "border" in the remaining steps.

10. Add the fringe following the directions in Adding the Fringe below. ***Note:*** *Fringed ends are optional in this project. If you choose not to add the fringe, you will have extra Single Strips to save for a future project. Refer to the information on Back-Up Strips on page 11 so they "blossom" to match the other strips in your projects.*

11. Working on the wrong side, pin and sew ***single strips*** to the outer edges of the scarf, sandwiching the raw edges of the scarf between two strips at the long edges and at the upper edges of the fringe strips as shown in Fig. 2.

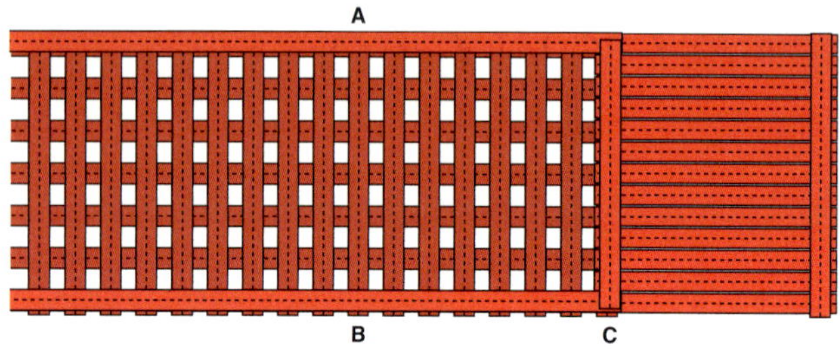

Fig. 2
Add strips A, B, and C, to sandwich strip ends.

12. Trim any loose threads. Place the fabric grid in the washing machine with an old towel or jeans. Wash and dry as directed on page 10, stopping twice during both cycles to remove the lint. If the scarf doesn't "blossom" as much as desired, repeat this step.

13. Use rotary-cutting tools to cut away the holding strips at the fringe ends.

14. Remove stray threads and lint by shaking the scarf outside, and then run a lint roller over it to remove any remaining lint. •

Adding the Fringe

1. Choose 26 strips, each at least 8 inches long. Stitch through the center of each strip and trim all strips to 8 inches long.

Note: *It is not necessary to perform this step on a tissue-paper or stabilizer grid.*

2. Position 13 strips on the wrong side at each end of the scarf and stitch to the border strips. (See Sew Like Knitting Fringe on page 11.)

3. To prevent the fringe strips from becoming tangled in the washing machine, place a ***Single Strip*** (a holding strip) across the lower ends of the fringe strips and stitch in place ¼ inch from the raw edges (Fig. 1a).

Note: *After washing and drying the completed scarf, cut off the holding strip at the end of the fringe using rotary-cutting equipment.*

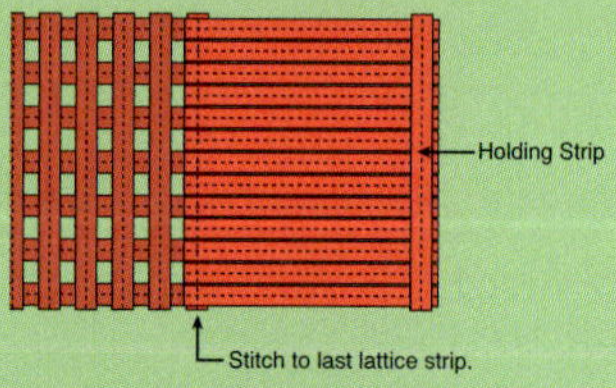

Fig. 1a
Add fringe strips to wrong side of scarf lattice.

Sampler Scarf

This project gives you an opportunity to test a number of the different stitch textures possible with the *Sew Like Knitting* technique. Just as in knitting, each variation is called a "stitch." Make it section-by-section—and then sew them together to make this easy scarf that is easier than it may look.

PROJECT SPECIFICATIONS

Finished Size: 7 x 92 inches, including fringe
Skill Level: Intermediate

MATERIALS

- 44/45-inch-wide osnaberg or a similar natural-fiber woven fabric
  - 1½ yards Fabric #1 (dusty rose)
  - ½ yard Fabric #2 (white)
  - ½ yard Fabric #3 (burgundy)
- Optional: 2 sheets *Sew Like Knitting Cutting Grid* and temporary spray adhesive
- 3 trays for fabric strips
- 1 sheet of *Sew Like Knitting Sewing Grid Type A* (1¼-inch squares) OR tissue paper or 1½ yards 23-inch-wide tear-away stabilizer and fine-tip pen and ruler
- All-purpose thread to match fabric
- Rotary cutter, mat and ruler
- Open-toe presser foot for sewing machine
- Clear cellophane tape
- Lint roller
- Basic sewing tools and equipment

BEFORE YOU BEGIN

The "stitches" in this sampler are created by sewing strips in the spaces between lattice strips in small sections that you make first. Refer to the directions below to complete each section. After you have completed all 13 lattice sections, following the specific directions for each one, you will sew the sections together to create the scarf.

INSTRUCTIONS

***Project Note:** You will use **Single Strips** and a few **Double Strips** in this project.*

Strip Preparation

1. Prepare each of the three fabrics by dividing each one into two equal pieces as directed in Step One on page 5. Cut each layered fabric into ⅝-inch-wide true-bias strips. Trim the ends as shown in Fig. 2 on page 6.

2. Separate all strips. Place all Fabric #1 strips in one tray. Place Fabric #2 and Fabric #3 strips on their individual trays.

***Note:** When **Double Strips** are specified in the materials list for a section of the scarf, layer two singles with raw edges even for each one.*

3. ***To use the Sew Like Knitting Sewing Grid Type A,*** cut 13 rectangles, each 7 x 8 squares. ***To make your own sewing grids,*** draw 13 (1¼-inch) grids, each 7 x 8 squares, on tissue paper or tear-away stabilizer. These sections will be referred to as "blocks" in the directions that follow.

4. Adjust the sewing machine for a 1.5mm stitch length and test the stitch length and tension as directed on page 8 before proceeding.

Even-Numbered Filler Blocks(Six)

Materials for Six Filler Blocks

- 12 (11-inch-long) *Single Strips* (A) Fabric #1 (dusty rose)
- 24 (11-inch-long) *Double Strips* (B) of Fabric #1
- 42 (10-inch-long) *Double Strips* (C) Fabric #1
- 6 grids (See step 3 of Strip Preparation, above.)

1. Working on one of the six grids: Pin a ***Single Strip (A)*** to the first and sixth lines and a ***Double Strip (B)*** to the lines in between the two outer lines. Beginning and ending the stitching on the excess strip that extends beyond the grid edges, stitch through the center of all strips. Remove the pins as you sew. Repeat to make a total of six grids.

2. Pin and sew ***Double Strips*** (C) to the remaining lines of the grid in the same manner. Repeat with each of the grids to complete the base lattice.

3. Remove the paper as directed in Step Four on page 9.

4. Using rotary-cutting tools, trim the edges so the lattice for each of the six blocks is 5 x 6 squares.

5. Set these blocks aside until you have assembled the remaining seven blocks and are ready to assemble the scarf.

Base Lattice for Odd-Numbered Blocks

You will need seven identical pieces of lattice to complete each of the remaining seven blocks for your scarf. Make each one following the steps below, then proceed to the directions for each block. You will add a different *Sew Like Knitting* "stitch" to each of the seven lattice sections to complete the odd-numbered blocks for your scarf.

Materials for Seven Base Lattice Sections

- 42 (11-inch-long) *Single Strips* (A) Fabric #1 (dusty rose)
- 49 (10-inch-long) *Single Strips* (B) Fabric #1 (dusty rose)
- 7 grids (see Step 3 of Strip Preparation, above)

1. Center, pin and sew a ***Single Strip (A)*** to each horizontal line on one of the grids.

2. Pin and sew ***Single Strips (B)*** to the remaining grid lines in the same manner.

3. Repeat steps 1 and 2 on each of the remaining six grids. Remove the grids as directed on page 9.

4. Using rotary-cutting tools, trim the edges so the lattice for each of the seven blocks is 5 x 6 squares.

5. Stack the lattice sections, orienting them so there are 6 squares across and 5 squares down. In other words, as you look at the stack of lattice on your work surface, there should be six vertical rows of squares. These are vertical spaces and the strips on either side are vertical strips.

From the top to the bottom of the lattice there should be five horizontal rows of squares creating five horizontal spaces between the horizontal lattice strips.

Note: *To keep the blocks correctly oriented for the vertical and horizontal references in the steps below, pin the stack together with a safety pin at the upper edge. Remove one piece of lattice at a time to complete each of the blocks required.*

Block 1: Stripe Stitch

Materials for Block 1

- 1 prepared base lattice (see above)
- 10 (10-inch-long) *Single Strips* Fabric #2 (white)

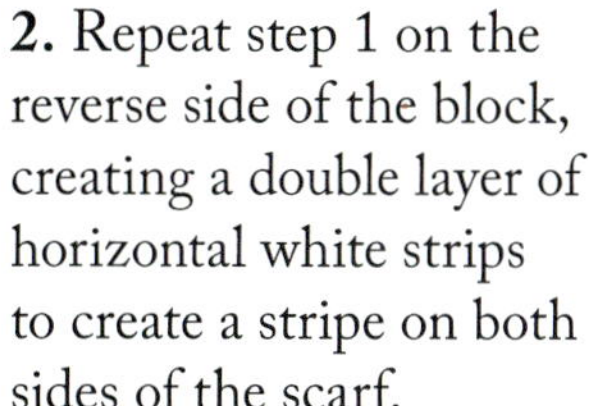

1. Pin and sew a ***Single Strip*** of Fabric #2 to the spaces between the strips on one side of the prepared lattice.

2. Repeat step 1 on the reverse side of the block, creating a double layer of horizontal white strips to create a stripe on both sides of the scarf.

3. Trim the ends of the strips even with outer edges of the scarf lattice. Set the completed block aside.

Block 3: Stained Glass Stitch

Materials for Block 3

- 1 prepared base lattice (see above)
- 6 (10-inch-long) *Single Strips* Fabric #3 (burgundy)
- 4 (10-inch-long) *Single Strips* Fabric #1 (dusty rose)

1. Pin and sew ***Single Strips*** of Fabric #3 in the spaces between the vertical strips of Fabric #1 on the grid.

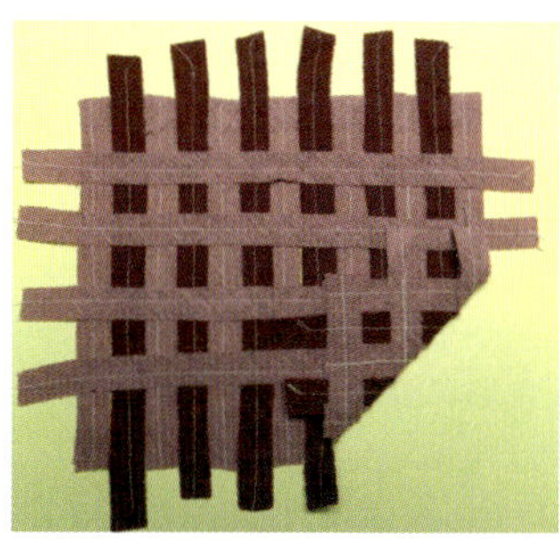

2. Pin and sew ***Single Strips*** of Fabric #1 across the grid in the remaining spaces.

3. Trim the ends of the Fabric #1 strips even with the outer edges of the scarf lattice. Set the completed block aside.

Block 5: Tricolored Stripe Stitch

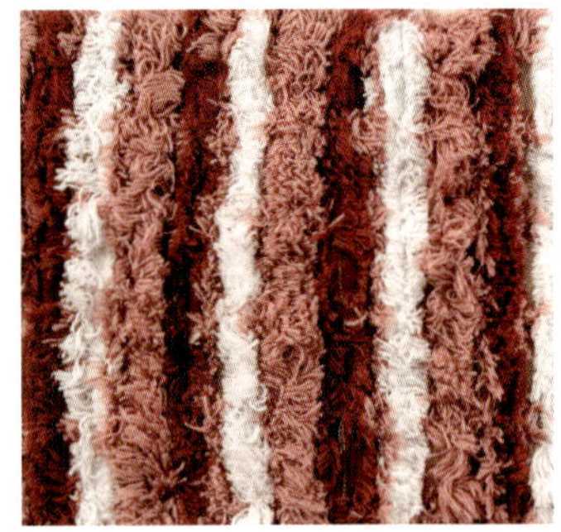

Materials for Block 5

- 1 prepared base lattice (see above)
- 8 (10-inch-long) *Single Strips* Fabric #2 (white)
- 8 (10-inch-long) *Single Strips* Fabric #3 (burgundy)
- 8 (10-inch-long) *Single Strips* Fabric #1 (dusty rose)

Note: *The pattern repeat is in numerical order (dusty rose, white, burgundy).*

1. Sew a ***Single Strip*** of Fabric #1 (dusty rose) to the first lattice strip at the left-hand edge of Block 5.

2. Working left to right across the lattice, sew a ***Single Strip*** of Fabric #3 (burgundy) in the space between the first two strips of the lattice Sew a ***Single Strip*** of Fabric #2 (white) on top of the next dusty rose strip.

3. Sew a dusty rose ***Single Strip*** in the next space and add a Fabric #3 (burgundy) ***Single Strip*** on top of the following strip.

4. Continue adding vertical strips in this manner to complete the striped pattern across the section, ending by adding a dusty rose strip to the strip at the right-hand edge of the section.

5. Turn the piece over and add strips in a similar fashion to repeat the pattern on the reverse side. ***Do not add a dusty rose strip to the two outermost strips, as these strips were already doubled in steps 1 and 5 above.*** Trim the strip ends even with the edges of the scaft lattice. Set the completed block aside.

Block 7: Duo Plaida Stitch

Materials for Block 7

- 1 prepared base lattice (see above)
- 11 (10-inch-long) *Single Strips* Fabric #2 (white)

1. Pin and sew ***Single Strips*** of Fabric #2 in the vertical spaces of the base lattice.

2. Pin and sew strips of Fabric #2 in the horizontal spaces of the base lattice. Trim strip ends even with the edge of the scarf lattice. Set the completed block aside.

Block 9: Confetti Stitch

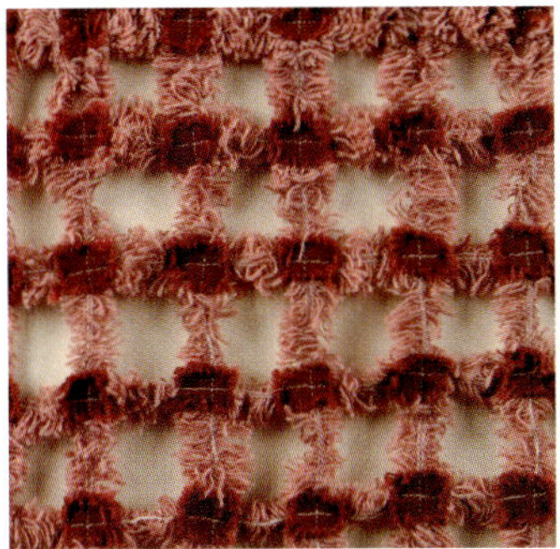

Materials for Block 9

- 1 prepared base lattice (see above)
- 84 (½-inch-long) strips Fabric #3 (burgundy)

1. Position one ½-inch-long strip at each intersection of the lattice for Block 9. Stitch across each strip with the stitching crossing each horizontal strip.

2. Repeat on the reverse side, with the stitches crossing the first confetti stitching so the stitches create a cross on each confetti piece.

Block 11: Herringbone Stitch

Materials for Block 11

- 1 prepared base lattice (see above)
- 12 (4-inch-long) strips Fabric #2 (white)

1. Stitch through the center of each of the 12 strips of Fabric #2 ***before applying them to the base lattice.***

2. With the exception of the left-hand vertical strip, position a strip of Fabric #2 at an angle at the upper edge of each vertical strip in the section and pin in place.

3. Pull each strip to the right and anchor the end at the next intersection to create the zigzag effect. Sew the strips in place across the width of the strips.

4. Repeat steps 2 and 3 to fill in the remaining section of the grid; notice that there is one open section between the two sets of herringbones.

Block 13: Irregular Tri-Plaida Stitch

Materials for Block 13

- 1 prepared base lattice (see above)
- 7 (10-inch-long) *Single Strips* Fabric #3 (burgundy)
- 4 (10-inch-long) *Single Strips* Fabric #2 (white)

Sampler Scarf

Note: When creating a plaid stitch with more than two colors, it is essential to position all of the vertical and then the horizontal strips (or vice versa) of one color ***before*** *proceeding to the next color. Otherwise the pattern of the plaid will be broken. In this project, Fabric #3 is the primary color and is sewn to the base lattice first.*

1. Working from left to right, pin and sew a ***Single Strip*** of Fabric #3 (burgundy) in the first, third, fourth and sixth lengthwise spaces (vertical spaces) from the left- to the right-hand edges of the section. Trim the strips even with the outer edges of the block.

2. Sew a ***Single Strip*** of Fabric #3 in the first, third and fifth horizontal spaces. Trim strips even with the lattice edges.

3. Pin and sew ***Single Strips*** of Fabric #2 (white) in the second and fifth lengthwise spaces that run from the top to the bottom of the lattice section. Trim strips even with the lattice edges.

4. Pin and sew ***Single Strips*** of Fabric #1 in the second and fourth horizontal spaces.

Scarf Assembly & Finishing

1. Arrange the blocks in numerical order (or the order you prefer) on a large flat surface.

2. Position the lower edge of Block 1 on top of the first strip at the top of Block 2 and pin in place. Stitch in place on top of the original stitching.

3. Position the upper edge of Block 3 on top of the lower edge of Block 2 and pin in place. Stitch.

4. Repeat steps 2 and 3 to join the remaining blocks in the same manner.

5. For the optional fringe, refer to the basic directions for fringe on page 11. Add fringe to only the short ends of the scarf.

6. Trim any loose threads. Place the completed scarf lattice in the washing machine with an old towel or jeans. Wash and dry as directed on page 9, stopping to remove lint twice during both cycles. If the scarf doesn't "blossom" as much as desired, repeat this step.

7. If you added fringe, trim the ends to remove the "holding strips."

8. Remove excess lint by shaking the scarf outside, and then run a lint roller over it to remove any remaining lint. •

Poncho Asymmetric

This lovely textured poncho has a flippy little collar built right into the construction process. It's an easy way to create a layered look with any outfit and adds comfy warmth on a cool day. Turn it around as shown above and on page 28 for an entirely different look.

PROJECT SPECIFICATIONS

Finished Size: One sizes fits most adults
Skill Level: Intermediate

MATERIALS

- 3¼-yards mint green 45-inch-wide osnaberg or similar woven natural-fiber fabric
- Optional: *Sew Like Knitting Cutting Grid* and temporary spray adhesive
- Tissue paper or 2 yards 23-inch-wide tear-away stabilizer and fine-tip pen and ruler OR 1 sheet of *Sew Like Knitting Cutting Grid Type A* (1¼-inch squares)
- Tray for strips
- All-purpose thread to match fabric
- Rotary cutter, mat and ruler
- Clear cellophane tape
- Lint roller
- Open-toe presser foot for sewing machines
- Basic sewing tools and equipment

INSTRUCTIONS

Project Notes: *This project requires* ***Single*** *(one layer) and* ***Double*** *(two layers)* ***Strips.*** *See Step One on page 5.*

1. Prepare the fabric by dividing it into two equal pieces as directed in Step One on page 5. Cut the layered fabric into ⅝-inch-wide true-bias strips. Trim the ends as shown in Fig. 2 on page 6.

2. Place the strips on a tray. When ***Single Strips*** are required, separate the layered strips. For ***Double Strips***, use the two-layer strips as cut.

3. ***To use the Sew Like Knitting Sewing Grid Type A,*** cut two pieces that are 18 x 28 squares each. ***To make your own sewing grids,*** draw 1¼-inch grids, each 18 x 28 squares, on tissue paper or tear-away stabilizer.

4. Adjust the sewing machine for a 1.5mm stitch length and test the stitch length and tension as directed on page 8.

5. Beginning at one short end, roll the grid lengthwise, so approximately 10 rows of squares are showing; pin the rolled layers together temporarily.

6. Center a ***Double Strip*** (two layers) along the second short line of the grid. ***Note:*** *All strips should extend at least 2 inches beyond the grid edges. Beginning and ending the stitching on the excess fabric strip beyond the edges of the rectangle, sew through the center of the strip.* Repeat with the remaining strips, leaving the last line on the grid uncovered as you did the first (Fig. 1).

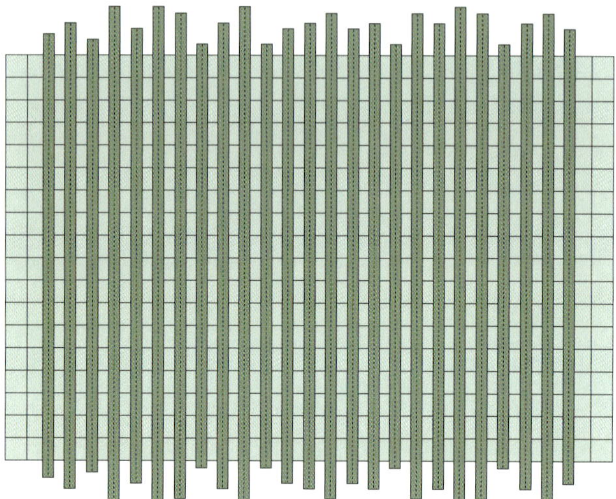

Fig. 1
Sew Double Strips to all grid lines except first and last.

7. Repeat step 6 to add ***Double Strips*** to each of the long lines on the grid (Fig. 2). When a strip is too short to cover the entire length of the line, simply overlap a new strip as shown in Fig. 6 on page 8 and continue stitching.

Fig. 2
Sew Double Strips to all but the first and last long line.

8. Repeat steps 5–7 with the second sewing grid.

9. Notice that there are spaces between each row of the resulting fabric lattice in both directions. On both pieces of lattice, pin and sew ***Single Strips*** in the spaces between the short rows as shown in Fig. 3.

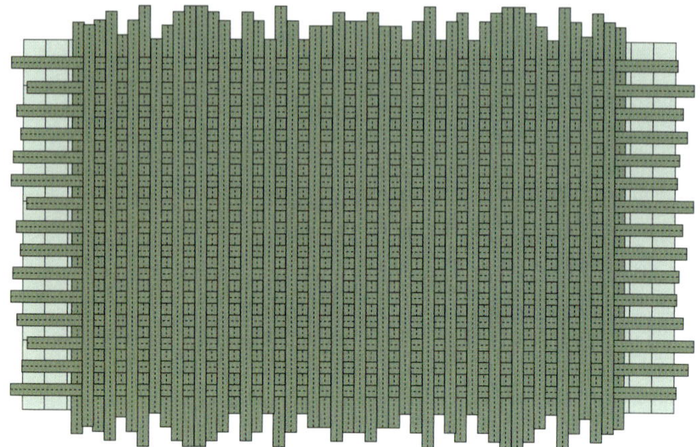

Fig. 3
Sew Single Strips in the spaces between the Short Strips.

10. Remove the paper as directed on page 9. Place a rectangle on the cutting mat and trim the excess at all four edges to 1½ inches. Repeat with the remaining rectangle.

11. Arrange the rectangles right side up and side by side on a large flat surface as shown in Fig. 4. Trim the excess 1½-inch built-in fringe from square 1 to square 8 at Side A and from square 8 to 26 on Side B. Trim the excess fringe from square #8 to square #16 on Side E and from square 8 to 26 on Side H.

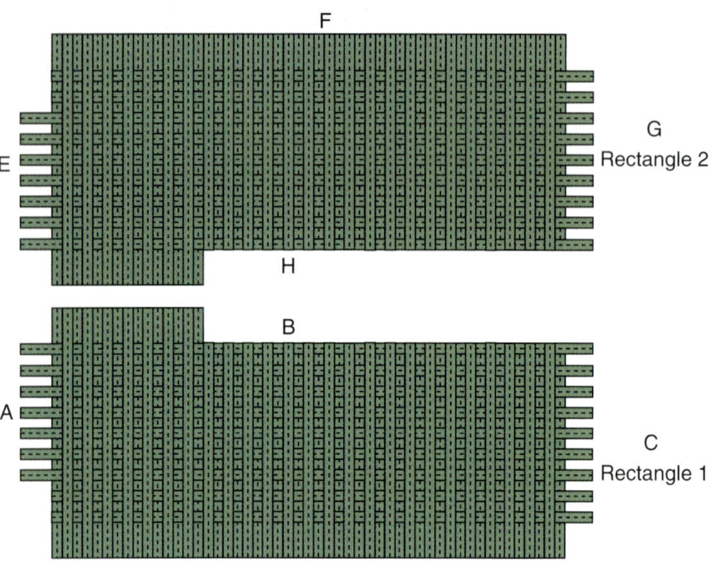

Fig. 4
Trim away fringe on edges A and E, and B and H as shown.

12. Position edge A on top of Edge E on Rectangle 2; pin in place (Fig. 5). Stitch through the center of the strips, backstitching at the beginning and end of the stitching.

13. Lap and stitch edge B over edge H in the same manner to complete the poncho construction. The opening is the neckline and the fringed corners fold down to create the built-in collar.

14. Wash and dry the poncho lattice as directed on page 10, stopping to remove lint twice during both cycles. If the poncho doesn't "blossom" as much as desired, repeat this step.

15. Remove excess lint by shaking the poncho outside and then run a lint roller over it. On a large project like this one, it may require an entire roll of lint-removing paper to lift all of the lint. ●

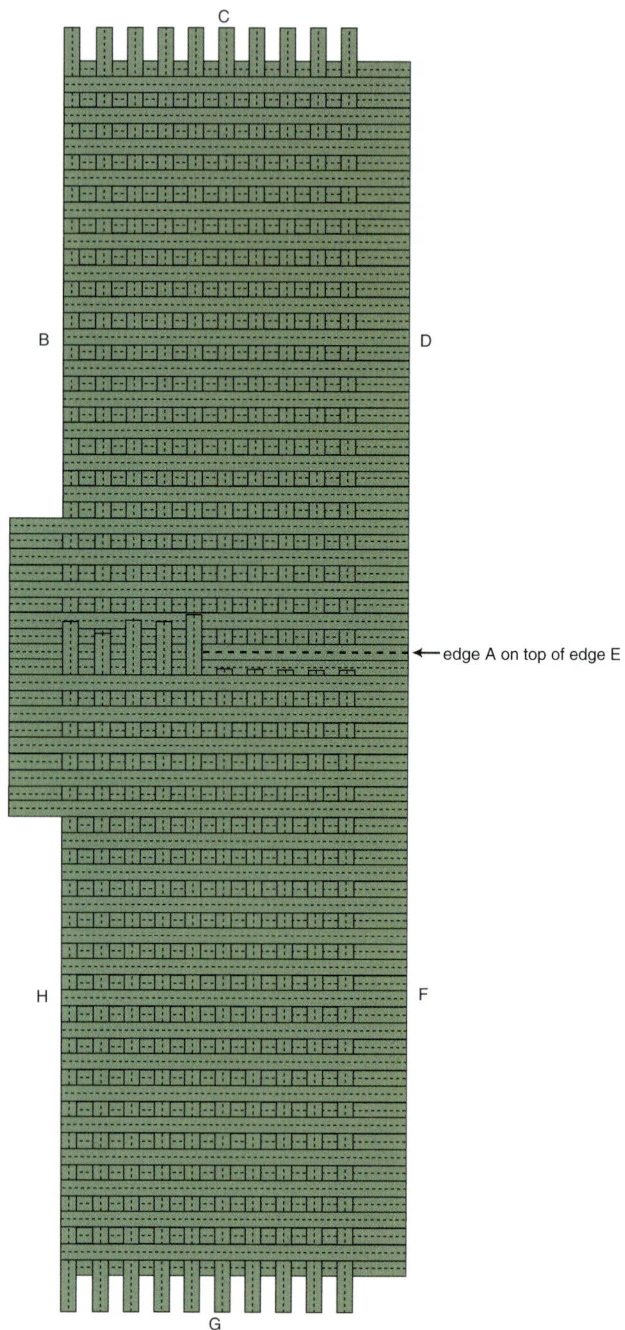

Fig. 5
Lap edge A over edge E and stitch.

Confetti Poncho

This poncho is made with an open lattice, similar to the Long & Lacy Scarf on page 17, with a twist. Small strips of different colors have been added to create the look of knitting with a variegated yarn. Use fewer colors for the confetti bits if you wish. It's really up to you.

PROJECT SPECIFICATIONS

Finished Size: **One sizes fits all**
Skill Level: **Intermediate**

MATERIALS

- 44/45-inch-wide cotton osnaberg or similar natural-fiber woven fabric
  - 2 yards Fabric #1 (light green)
  - ¼ yard each of four contrasting colors (red, natural, white, pine green)
- Optional: *Sew Like Knitting Sewing Grid* and temporary spray adhesive
- Rotary cutter, mat and ruler
- 2 trays for fabric strips
- Tissue paper or 2 yards of 23-inch-wide tear-away stabilizer and fine-tip pen and ruler OR 1 sheet of *Sew Like Knitting Sewing Grid Type A* (1¼-inch squares)
- All-purpose thread to match fabric
- Clear cellophane tape
- Lint roller
- Open-toe presser foot for sewing machine
- Basic sewing tools and equipment

INSTRUCTIONS

Project Notes: *All bias strips in this project are* ***Single Strips****. See Step One on page 5.*

1. Prepare each of the fabrics for cutting as directed in Step One on page 6. Cut each set of layered fabrics into ⅝-inch-wide strips.

2. Trim the ends of each strip of Fabric #1 as shown in Fig. 2 on page 6. Separate the strips into ***Single Strips*** and place them on one of the trays.

3. Cut the accent colors into ½-inch-long pieces and place each color in a separate pile on the second tray.

4. ***To use Sew Like Knitting Sewing Grid Type A,*** cut two rectangles each 16 x 28 squares. ***To make your own sewing grid,*** draw a 16 x 28 grid of 1¼-inch squares on two pieces of tissue paper or tear-away stabilizer.

5. Adjust the sewing machine for a 1.5mm stitch length and test the tension as directed on page 8.

6. Beginning at one short end, roll each grid so approximately 10 grid lines are showing. Pin the rolled layers together temporarily.

7. Center and stitch a Fabric #1 (light green) ***Single Strip*** on each exposed short grid line, beginning and ending the stitching on the excess fabric strip extending beyond the edges of the sewing grid. Unpin and unroll the grid to expose 10 more lines; re-pin. Sew the exposed strips in place. Continue in this fashion until all short lines are covered with strips (Fig. 1).

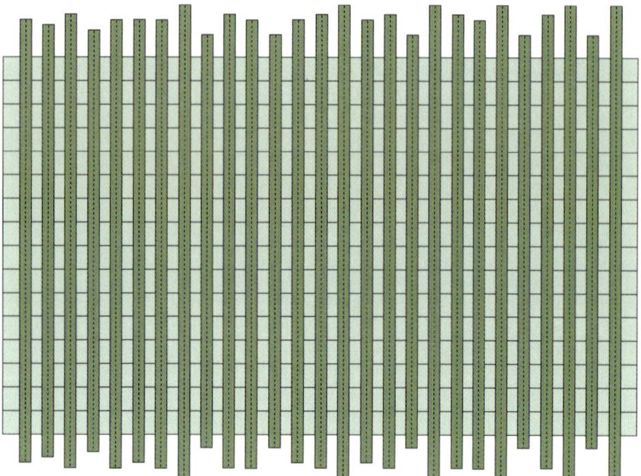

Fig. 1
Center and stitch Single Strips to short grid lines.

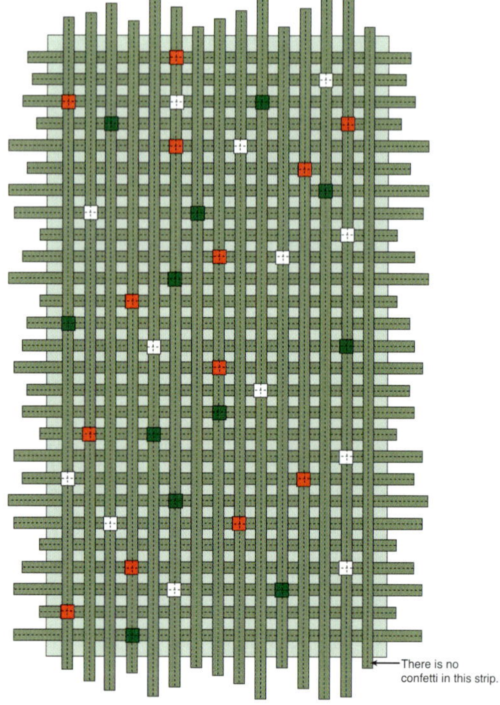

Fig. 2
Center and sew Single Strips to long grid lines with confetti bits at intersections.

8. Place a rectangle face up on a large flat surface. Center a Fabric #1 strip on each vertical line on the grid. Before pinning, add a short contrasting strip at each intersection—or at intermittent intersections as shown in Fig. 2 for a more random variegated look. Pin all strips in place through all fabric layers and the grid. ***Note:*** *Do not add confetti bits to the intersection along the grid line at the right-hand edge of the rectangle.*

9. Sew through the center of each strip, catching the confetti bits in the stitching and beginning and ending the stitching in the excess strip beyond each short end of the sewing grid. Repeat steps 8 and 9 with the remaining rectangle.

10. Remove the paper grid from both rectangles as directed in Step Four on page 9.

11. Place each rectangle on the cutting mat and trim the ends and edges so the resulting rectangles are 14 x 26 squares. Label the pieces Rectangle 1 and Rectangle 2, placing the tags in the strips that have no confetti bits. Then label the edges from A to H as shown in Fig. 3.

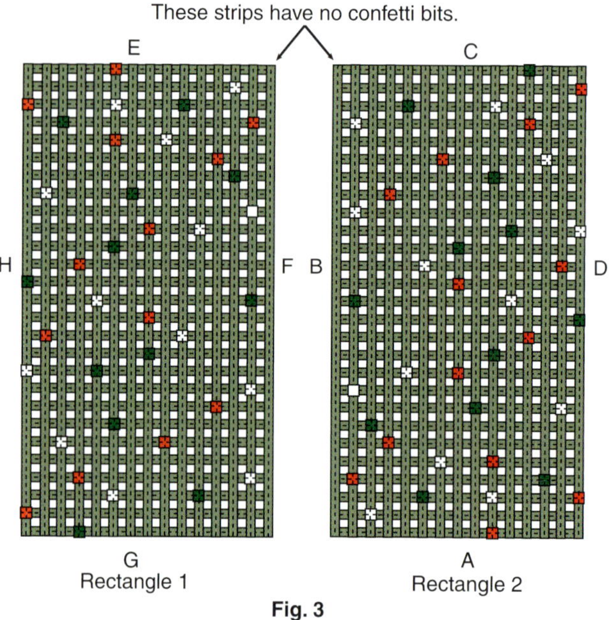

Fig. 3
Trim and label poncho lattice panels.

12. Turn the rectangles over and sew a ***Single Strip*** (border strip) to edges A, D, E, H only. Sew a border strip to the wrong side of edges B and F from square 14–26 only.

13. Place both rectangles right side up on a large flat surface, overlapping edge G on edge B from squares 1–14 (Fig. 4). Make sure the rows match and stitch through all layers on top of previous stitching; backstitch at the beginning and end of the stitching.

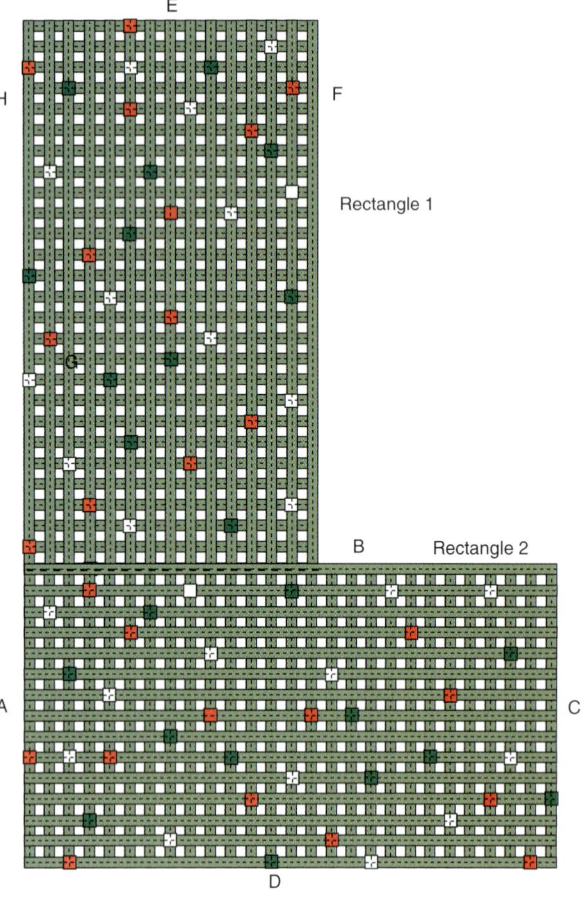

Fig. 4
Lap edge G over edge B
and stitch in place.

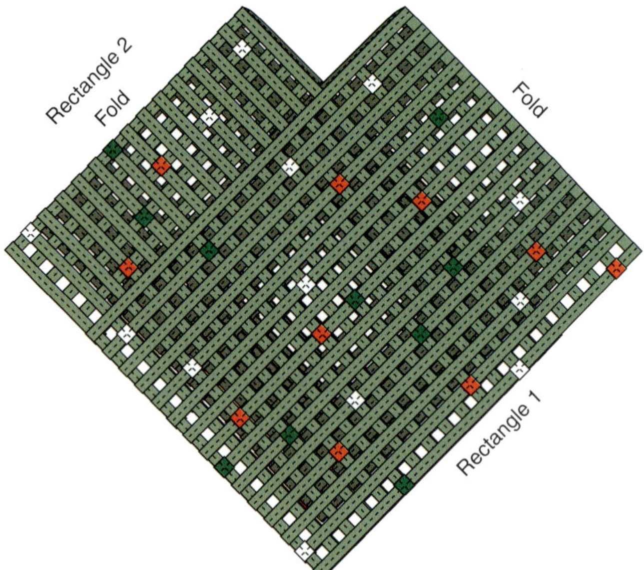

Fig. 5
Stitch remaining short edge
to opposite long edge (C to F).

14. Lap edge C over edge E, pin and stitch to complete the lattice for the poncho (Fig. 5). Trim any loose threads.

15. Wash and dry the completed poncho lattice as directed on page 10, stopping to remove lint twice during both cycles. If the poncho doesn't "blossom" as much as desired, repeat this step.

16. Remove excess lint by shaking the poncho outside and then run a lint roller over it to remove any remaining lint. On a large piece like this you may use the entire roll of paper on the roller. ●

Multicolor Striped Wrap

This luxurious wrap is a wonderful way to show off bold and beautiful stripes. The design has built-in fringe and the "stitch" is a variation of the Tri-Colored Stripe Stitch used in the Sampler Scarf on page 24. You will make a two-colored lattice before adding the strips to both sides of the lattice to create the stripes. Follow the directions carefully.

PROJECT SPECIFICATIONS

Finished Size: One sizes fits all
Skill Level: Intermediate

MATERIALS

- 44/45-inch-wide cotton osnaberg or similar natural-fiber woven fabric
  - 1½ yards Fabric #1 (dark blue)
  - 1 yard each of three contrasting colors for Fabrics #2, #3 and #4 (light blue, white and light green)
- Optional: 2 sheets of *Sew Like Knitting Sewing Grid* and temporary spray adhesive
- Rotary cutter, mat and ruler
- 4 trays for fabric strips
- Tissue paper or 2 yards 23-inch-wide stabilizer and a fine-tip pen and ruler OR 1 sheet of *Sew Like Knitting Sewing Grid Type A*
- All-purpose thread to match fabric (choose one color)
- Clear cellophane tape
- Lint roller
- Open-toe presser foot for sewing machine
- Basic sewing tools and equipment

INSTRUCTIONS

Project Notes: *This project requires* ***Single*** *(one-layer) and* ***Double*** *(two-layer) Strips. See Step One on page 5.*

1. Prepare each of the fabrics for cutting and cut each layered fabric into ⅝-inch-wide strips as directed in Step One on page 5. Trim the ends of all strips as shown in Fig. 2 on page 6.

2. Place the strips of each color on separate trays.

3. ***To use Sew Like Knitting Sewing Grid Type A,*** cut one rectangle that is 14 x 42 squares and a second rectangle that is 14 x 32 squares. ***To make your own sewing grids,*** draw 1¼-inch grids of the two sizes specified above on sheets of tissue paper or tear-away stabilizer. Overlap and tape the two grids together so the completed sewing grid is 14 squares wide and 73 squares long.

4. Adjust the sewing machine for a 1.5mm stitch length and test the stitch length and tension as directed on page 8.

5. Beginning at one short end, roll the grid, so approximately 10 short grid lines are showing; pin the rolled layers together temporarily.

6. Position and sew ***Double Strips*** of Fabric #1 (dark blue) on every other line from lines 5 through 69, ***leaving the first four and the last four grid lines uncovered.*** Begin and end the stitching on the excess fabric strip beyond the edges of the sewing grid (Fig. 1).

7. Sew ***Single Strips*** of Fabric #1 to every other long line, beginning with line 1 as shown in Fig. 2 (a total of seven strips). Overlap strips by at least ½ inch as shown in Fig. 1 when one strip is not long enough to cover an entire line.

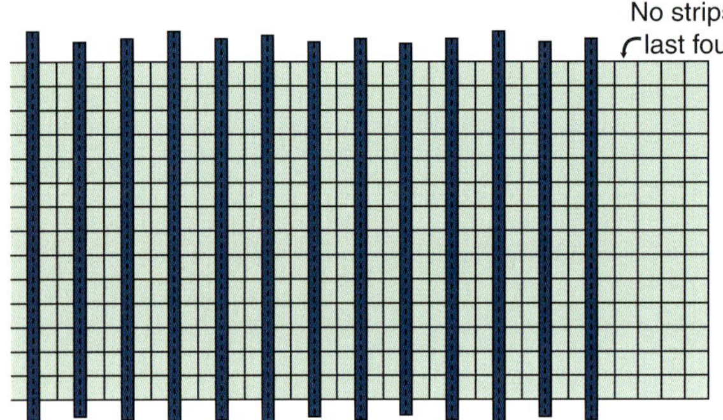

Fig. 1
Sew Double Strips to every other short grid line.

Fig. 2
Sew Single Strips to every other long grid line.

8. Add ***Single Strips*** of Fabric #2 (light blue) to the remaining six lines of the grid (Fig. 3).

Fig. 3
Sew Single Strips of Fabric #2 to the remaining long lines of grid.

9. Remove the paper or stabilizer as directed in Step 4 on page 9. Place the rectangle on the cutting mat and trim the excess strips that extend past the long edges of the rectangle. ***Do not trim the short ends, as they will become the fringe.***

10. Place the piece face up on a large flat surface. Pin ***Single Strips*** of Fabric #4 (light green) in the spaces between every second set of strips of Fabrics #1 and #2; you will add a total of six strips of Fabric #4 (Fig. 4). Make sure that each strip is as long as the strips of Fabrics 1 and 2 that extend beyond the grid edges for the fringe. Stitch in place through the center of the strips, beginning and ending the stitching on the strip extensions.

11. With the piece face up on the pinning surface, pin ***Single Strips*** of Fabric #3 (white) in the remaining spaces—a total of six strips (Fig. 5). Stitch in place through the center of the strips, beginning and ending the stitching on the extensions.

12. Turn the lattice wrong side up on the pinning surface. Note that the short strips of the lattice foundation still show on this side.

13. Add ***Singles*** of Fabrics #2, #3, and #4 on top of the first ones to create an identical striped pattern on the reverse side and hide the short lattice strips.

14. To prevent the fringe from tangling in the washing machine and dryer, position a ***Single Strip*** across the fringe ends and stitch through the center (see the sidebar on page 18).

15. Wash and dry the completed lattice, as directed on page 10, stopping to remove lint twice during both cycles. If the striped wrap doesn't "blossom" as much as desired, repeat this step.

16. Trim away the holding strips at each fringed end. Remove excess lint by shaking the wrap outside and then run a lint roller over it to remove any remaining lint. On a large piece like this, you may use the entire roll of paper on the roller.

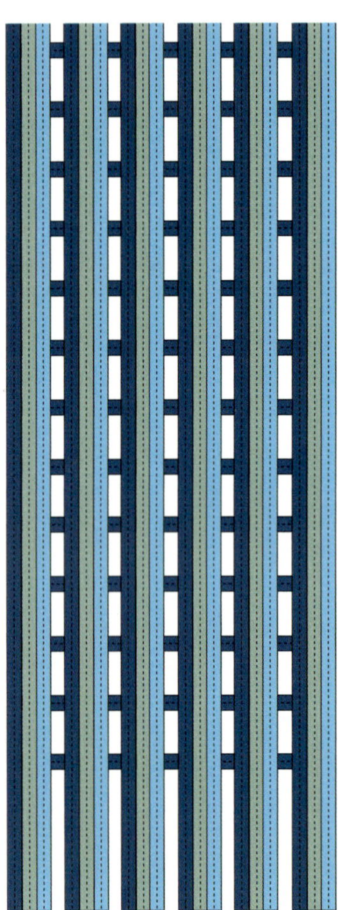

Strips have been trimmed even with long edges.

Fig. 4
Sew Single Strips of Fabric #4 in the spaces shown.

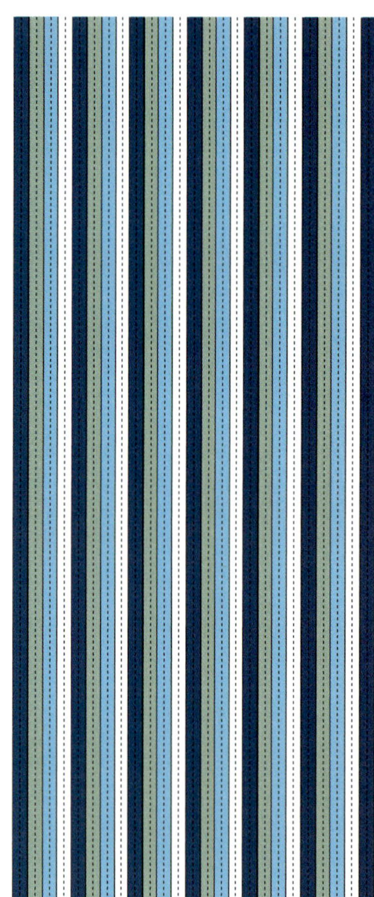

Fig. 5
Sew Single Strips of Fabric #3 in the remaining spaces.

A Little Shrug

Make this little shrug to wear when you need more coverage over bare or sleeveless styles. This is one wrap that can't fall off, no matter how active you are, and it starts as a simple rectangle. You can also use the shrug as a chunky scarf as shown above, and if you don't stitch the undearm seams, you will have a lovely shawl.

PROJECT SPECIFICATIONS

Finished Size: One size fits most average adults
Skill Level: Confident beginner

MATERIALS

- 2 yards 45-inch-wide red osnaberg or similar woven natural-fiber fabric
- Optional: 2 sheets *Sew Like Knitting Cutting Grid* and temporary spray adhesive
- Rotary cutter, mat and ruler
- All-purpose thread to match fabric
- Tissue paper or 2 yards of 23-inch-wide tear-away stabilizer and a fine-tip pen and ruler OR 1 sheet of *Sew Like Knitting Cutting Grid Type A*
- Tray for fabric strips
- Clear cellophane tape
- Lint roller
- Open-toe presser foot for sewing machine
- Basic sewing tools and equipment

INSTRUCTIONS

Project Notes: *This project requires* ***Single Strips****. See Step One on page 5.*

1. Prepare the fabric for cutting and cut the layered fabric into ⅝-inch-wide strips as directed in Step One on page 6.

2. Trim the ends of all strips as shown in Fig. 2 on page 6. Separate the double-layer cut strips into ***Single Strips*** and place the strips on the tray.

3. ***To use Sew Like Knitting Sewing Grid Type A,*** cut two rectangles each 12 x 24 squares. Tape the two grids together overlapping by one row of squares at the short ends to create a 12 x 47-square grid. ***To make your own sewing grids,*** draw a 1¼-inch grid of 12 x 47 squares on the tissue paper or stabilizer.

4. Adjust the sewing machine for a 1.5 stitch length and test the stitch length and tension as directed on page 8.

5. Roll the grid from one short end, leaving 10 grid lines showing and pin the layers temporarily. Sew ***Single Strips*** to every short grid line, beginning and ending on the excess fabric strip beyond the edges of the sewing grid (Fig. 1 on page 40). Unroll and pin the grid as needed to complete all short lines.

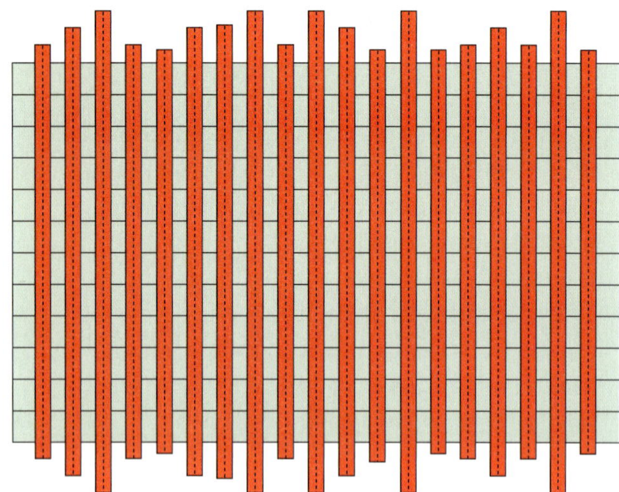

Fig. 1
Sew short Single Strips to the grid.

6. Position and sew a ***Single Strip*** to every long grid line (Fig. 2). If strips are not long enough to completely cover a line, overlap a new strip as shown in Fig. 6 on page 8 and complete the line.

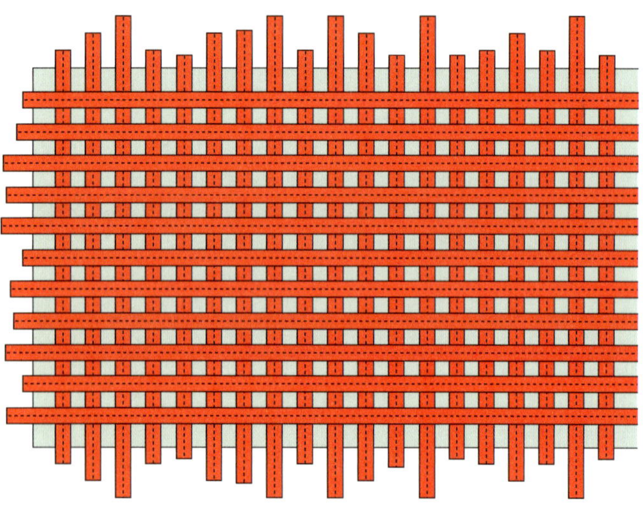

Fig. 2
Sew Single Strips to complete the lattice grid.

7. Remove the paper as directed on page 9.

8. Position and pin a ***Single Strip*** over each space between two short rows of lattice, making sure that it extends beyond the edges of the lattice like the first strips do (Fig 3). Stitch each strip in place through the center from one end to other, just as you did with all of the lattice strips.

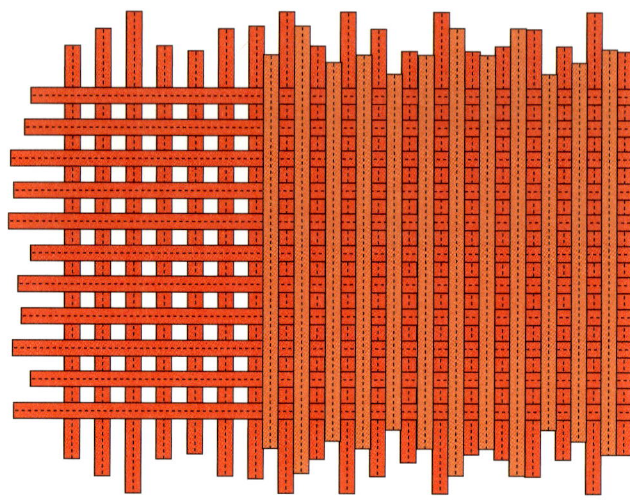

Fig. 3
Sew Single Strips in the short spaces of the lattice (shown in different color for clarity).

9. Place the completed lattice on the cutting mat and trim so the finished rectangle is 10 x 45 squares (refer to Fig. 4 on page 42).

10. Wash and dry the completed lattice as directed on page 10, stopping to remove lint twice during both cycles. If the piece doesn't "blossom" as much as desired, repeat this step.

11. Remove excess lint by shaking the piece outside and then run a lint roller over it to remove any remaining lint. On a large piece like this you may use all the paper on the roll.

12. Place the piece right side up on a large, flat surface with one long edge at the top. Measure 17 inches from each short end and mark the "underarms" at both long edges (Fig. 4).

13. Fold the rectangle in half with the right sides together and pin the edges together, ending at the 17-inch marks, to create the "sleeves." Place the pins parallel to the long edge with the pins pointing to the short ends so that you can try on the shrug, as pinned, to test the size. Carefully slip your arms through the pinned sections—the sleeves. If the shrug feels too tight across the back or under the arms, remove a pin at each side and try it on again. Removing one pin at each side will add about 1 inch across the back. Continue adjusting the pins as needed until you have a comfortable fit. Sew the layers together through the outer border strips (Fig. 5).

14. Turn the shrug right side out, tuck your arms into the sleeves and just try to shrug this one off! •

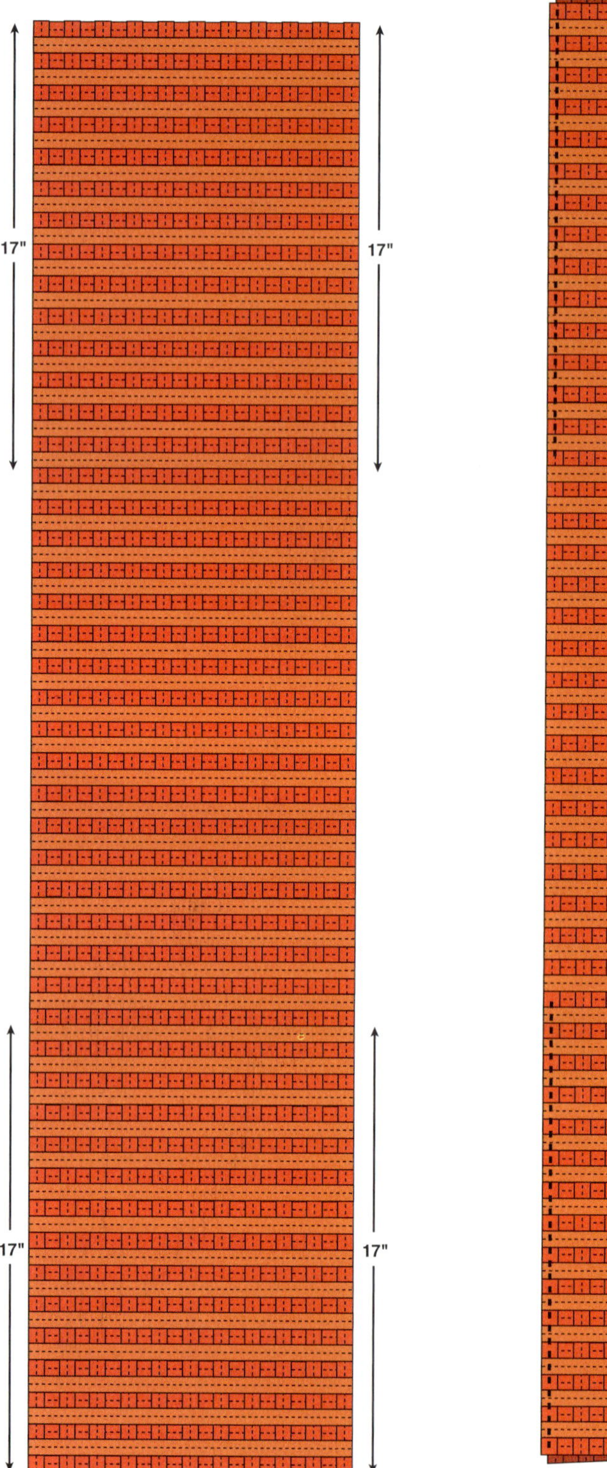

Fig. 4
Mark "underarms" for the seam.

Fig. 5
Stitch with right sides together as pinned to fit.

Variegated Plaid Poncho

This traditionally shaped poncho is the perfect project for combining fabrics in your favorite colors. Imagine it in shades of pink, red and lavender instead of these sky blue colors. Your finished poncho will be uniquely yours. Wear it your way—with a V-neckline or a boat neckline as shown above.

PROJECT SPECIFICATIONS

Finished Size: One size fits most adults
Skill Level: Experienced

MATERIALS

- 1 yard each of four colors of 45-inch-wide cotton osnaberg or other similar woven natural-fiber fabric (navy, teal, green and white) or leftover strips of at least 4 colors
- Optional: 2 sheets of *Sew Like Knitting Sewing Grid* and temporary spray adhesive
- Rotary cutter, mat and ruler
- All-purpose thread to match fabric (choose 1 color)
- Tissue paper or 2 yards of 23-inch-wide tear-away stabilizer and a fine-point pen and ruler OR 1 sheet of *Sew Like Knitting Sewing Grid Type A*
- Tray for fabric strips
- Clear cellophane tape
- Lint roller
- Open-toe presser foot for sewing machine
- Basic sewing tools and equipment

INSTRUCTIONS

Project Notes: *This project requires* ***Single Strips.*** *See Step One on page 5.*

1. Prepare each of the fabrics for cutting and cut each layered fabric into ⅝-inch-wide strips as directed in Step One on page 5. Trim the ends of all strips as shown in Fig. 2 on page 6.

2. Cut the strips into assorted lengths, none longer than 12 inches or shorter than 2 inches. Separate the strips into ***Single Strips***. Mix colors and strip lengths and place on the tray.

3. ***To use Sew Like Knitting Sewing Grid Type A,*** cut a 32 x 32-square grid. ***To make your own sewing grid,*** draw a 1¼-inch grid, 32 x 32 squares, on tissue paper or tear-away stabilizer. Mark the edges of the grid as shown in (Fig. 1 on page 44).

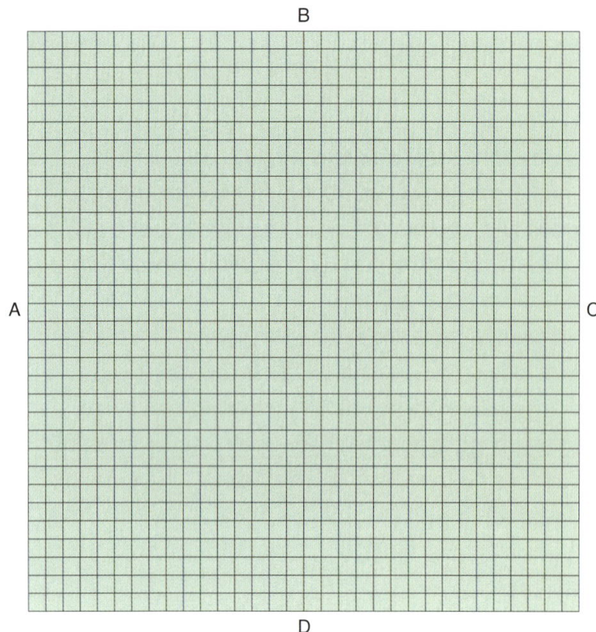

Fig. 1
Make sewing grid and label edges.

4. Fold the square in half diagonally. At the center of the folded line, measure and mark 6 inches to each side of center for the neckline opening (Fig. 2).

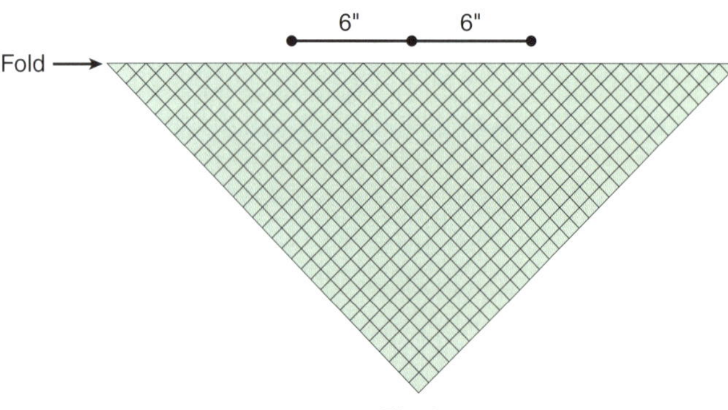

Fig. 2
Mark neckline at center fold.

5. Open the square and draw a 12-inch-long line for the neckline between the two marks. Transfer the line to the wrong side of the grid, too.

6. Adjust the sewing machine to a 1.5mm stitch length and test the stitch length and tension as directed on page 8.

7. Place the sewing grid right side up on a large flat surface. Working from edge A to edge C, center and pin ***Single Strips*** in place on the grid lines in a random arrangement of colors and strip lengths. Place all pins so they point to Edge A. When you add the next short strip to a line, overlap it by at least ½ inch and pin in place (Fig. 3). Continue adding strips in this fashion to cover the lines in this direction with randomly arranged strips.

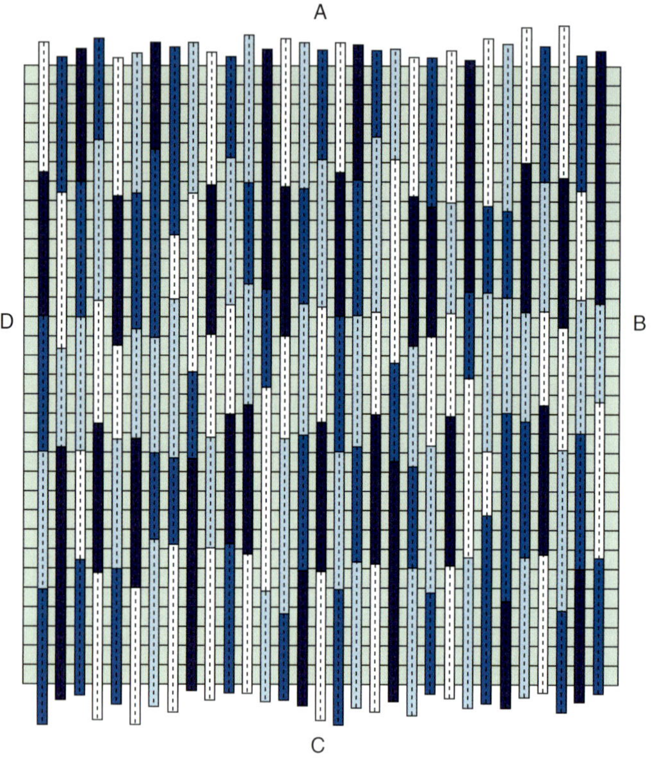

Fig. 3
Pin and sew strips in one direction.

8. Beginning at edge D, roll the pinned sewing grid so that only five rows are showing and the pins point to the sewing machine. Stitch through the center of each row of strips, removing the pins as you go. Unpin and unroll to expose the remaining rows to complete the square.

9. Repeat steps 7 and 8 to cover the remaining grid lines with assorted colors and lengths of ***Single Strips*** that cross the first set of strips (Fig. 4)

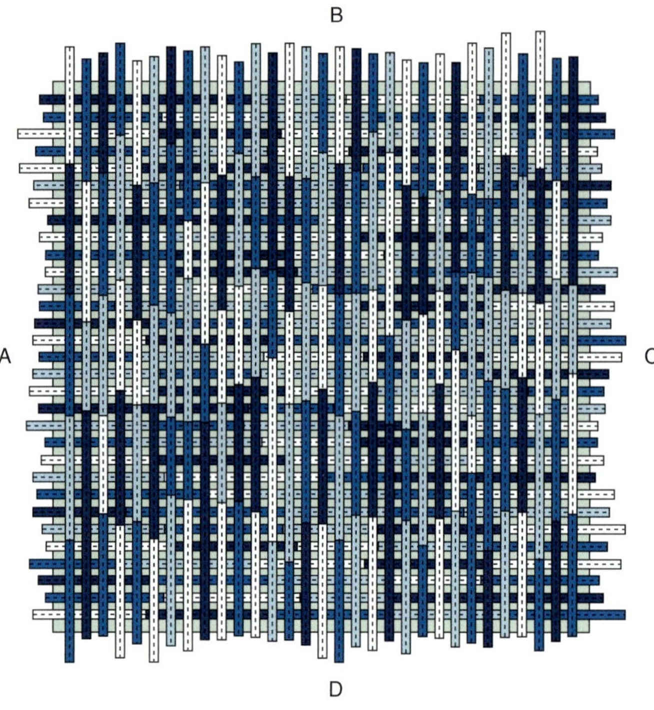

Fig. 4
Add strips to the remaining grid lines.

10. Trim the excess strip ends even with the grid edges all around. Turn the grid over and carefully cut along the line you drew for the neckline opening. It will designated in the following illustrations as shown in Fig. 5.

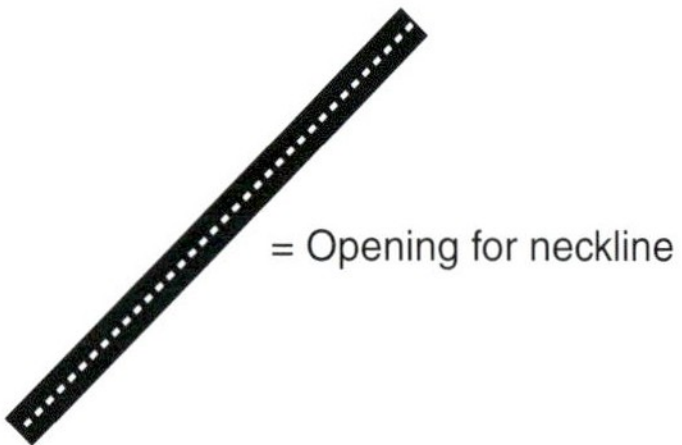

Fig. 5
Neckline Opening

11. Remove the paper or stabilizer as directed in Step Four on page 9.

12. Place the fabric grid face up on a large, flat surface. Pin strips in place over the spaces between the lattice strips from Edge A to Edge C. Make sure that the strips extend the same length as the already-stitched strips at each edge. Stitch in place (Fig. 6).

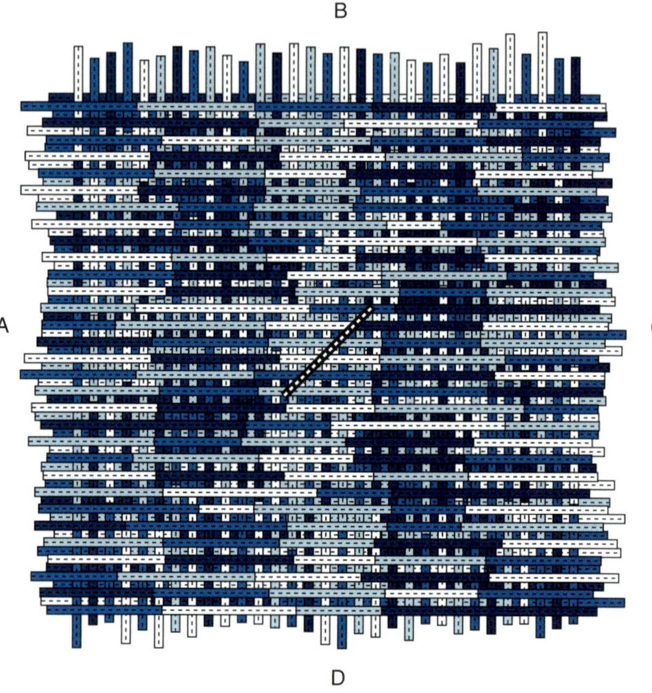

Fig. 6
Add strips to the A – C spaces between the strips.

13. Repeat step 12 to add random strip lengths and colors to the remaining open spaces in the lattice as seen in Fig. 7.

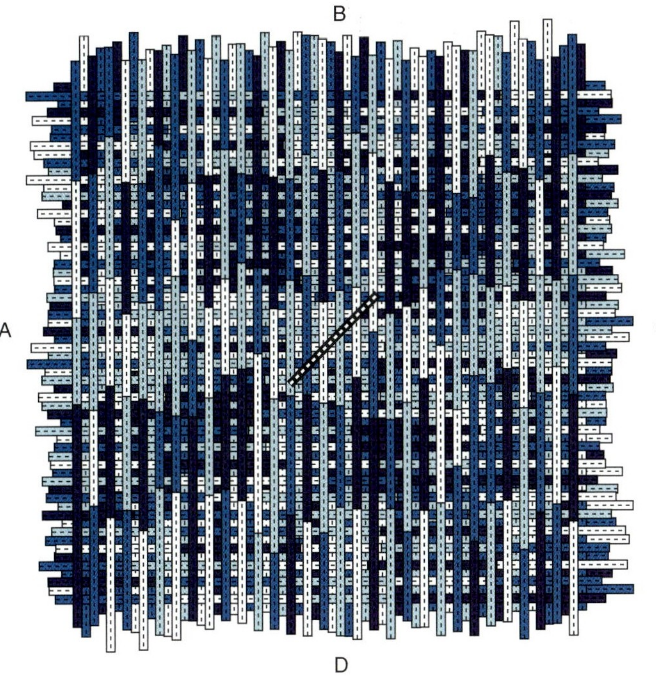

Fig. 7
Add strips to the remaining spaces.

14. Position the completed lattice on the cutting board. Trim excess strips even with Edges A and C. Repeat with Edges B and D (Fig. 8).

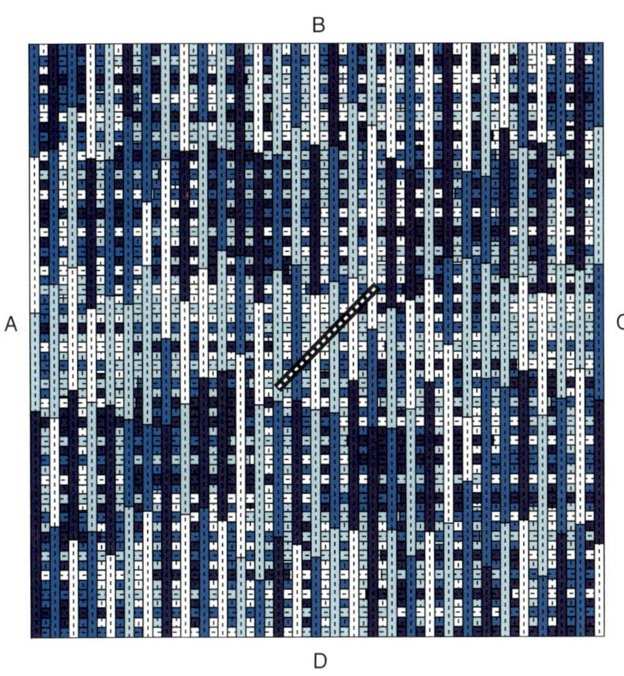

Fig. 8
Trim excess even with edges of lattice.

15. Pin and sew a ***Single Strip*** to the right side of the lattice at all four outer edges, creating a border.

16. Cut four ***Single Strips*** each 13 inches long and 4 single strips each 1 inch long for the neckline border. *On the right side of the lattice,* pin a 13-inch strip to each neckline cut edge with ½ inch of each strip extending past the cut at each end. Repeat on the wrong side. Position a 1-inch-long strip across the short ends of the strips at each end of the neckline on both sides of the poncho. Stitch through all layers at the center of each strip (Fig. 9).

Fig. 9
Stitch strips to neckline opening edges (lattice not shown).

17. Wash and dry the poncho lattice as directed on page 10, stopping to remove the lint twice during both cycles. If the poncho doesn't "blossom" as much as desired, repeat this step.

18. Remove excess lint by shaking the poncho outside and then run a lint roller over it to remove any remaining lint. You will probably use up the entire roll of paper on this large piece. ●

Sew Like Knitting is published by Clotilde/DRG Publishing, 306 East Parr Road, Berne, IN 46711, telephone (260) 589-4000. Printed in USA.

RETAILERS: If you would like to carry this pattern book or any other DRG publications, call the WholesaleDepartment to set up a direct account: (903) 636-4303. Also, request a complete listing of publications available.

Editor: Barbara Weiland
Associate Editor: Dianne Schmidt
Technical Artist: Nicole Gage
Copy Supervisor: Michelle Beck
Copy Editors: Nicki Lehman, Beverly Richardson
Art Director: Brad Snow

Assistant Art Director: Nick Pierce
Graphic Production Supervisor: Ronda Bechinski
Graphic Artist: Jessi Butler
Photography: Scott Campbell, Christena Green
Photo Stylist: Martha Coquat

ISBN: 0-9748217-2-1 Printed in U.S.A. 1 2 3 4 5 6 7 8 9